THE **FBI** AND THE **CIA**

SECRET AGENTS AND

☆ ─────────────────────────────────────

Illustrated with photographs

THE

FBİ

AND THE

CİA

AMERICAN DEMOCRACY

JAMES MUNVES

HARCOURT BRACE JOVANOVICH

NEW YORK AND LONDON

B C D E F G H I J K

Library of Congress Cataloging in Publication Data

Munves, James.
    The FBI and the CIA: secret agents and American democracy.

    Bibliography: p.
    Includes index.
    SUMMARY: Presents cases involving the FBI and
the CIA from the Depression years to the Watergate
burglary and discusses the role of these two
agencies in government and in the lives of ordinary
citizens.
    1. United States. Federal Bureau of Investi-
gation—Juvenile literature.   2. United States.
Central Intelligence Agency—Juvenile literature.
[1. United States. Federal Bureau of Investigation.   2. United States. Central Intelligence
Agency]   I. Title.
HV8138.M84   353.007′4   75-10136
ISBN 0-15-227423-5

Contents

THE **FBI** AND THE **CIA**

1

Every word [of the Constitution] decides a question between power and liberty. —JAMES MADISON in the *National Gazette,* January 19, 1792

Lew Erskine, James Bond, and the Constitution

In the early hours of September 26, 1933, FBI agents and local police silently closed in on a small bungalow in Memphis, Tennessee.

Through a window they could see their quarry, the notorious bandit George "Machine-gun" Kelly. Beside Kelly, on the dining-room table, was an automatic pistol. Several loaded submachine guns lay on the floor.

At six in the morning, after Kelly had gone to sleep, they sneaked into the house. When Kelly opened his bedroom door, a gun in his hand, a shotgun was shoved in his belly. "Don't shoot, G-men," Kelly pleaded. "Don't shoot."

News of Kelly's capture revealed to the public the new name, *G-men,* the underworld had given to the special agents of the Federal Bureau of Investigation, which was then engaged in a spectacular war on crime.

The FBI had tracked Kelly down by clean, scientific detective work. The chase had started just two months before when Charles F. Urschel, a wealthy Oklahoma oil man, was kidnapped. When he was released, after payment of $200,000 ransom, Urschel gave the FBI a number of clues.

About nine hours after he was kidnapped, as he lay on the floor in the back of the car, Urschel heard the lady filling his captor's gas tank say, "The crops around here are burned up, although we may make some broom corn."

He was kept, blindfolded and handcuffed, in a house where he heard chickens, hogs, and cows. He heard water drawn from a well, which he guessed was northwest of the house. The water, which he took from a tin cup without a handle, had a strong mineral taste. He also managed to move his blindfold enough to read his watch and in this way checked the times he heard a plane pass over the house every morning and evening. On Sunday, July 30, it rained hard and he didn't hear the morning plane.

The FBI men went to work on these clues. By checking airline schedules and weather records, they calculated that Urschel had been kept in a house in the vicinity of Paradise, Texas.

Checking the area, they found a ranch house with chickens, hogs, and cows that had a well with a tin cup missing a handle. When they brought Urschel to look the place over, he recognized the taste of the water and then found the chain to which his handcuffs had been fastened.

The house, which belonged to the parents of "Machinegun" Kelly's wife, Kathryn, put the FBI on the trail of the kidnappers. With untiring persistence the agents found the criminals and risked death in capturing Kelly and his arsenal of weapons. The image of the scourge of the police forces of a dozen states cringing before the G-men delighted the public.

Ten months later, on July 22, 1934, at 10:30 P.M., a slender, middle-sized man wearing silver-rimmed glasses stepped out of the Biograph Theater in East Chicago, where he had just seen one of his favorite actors, Clark Gable, in the gangster movie *Manhattan Melodrama*. Blinking beneath the lights of the marquee, he sensed something was amiss and raced for a near-by alleyway, trying to draw a gun from his pocket. Before he could pull the trigger, he was dead, pierced by two bullets. Fifteen G-men had caught John Herbert Dillinger, the leader of a gang that had terrorized the Midwest, plundering police arsenals, liberating prisoners, robbing banks, and murdering or maiming seventeen victims.

During the depression years of the 1930s, the G-men tracked down Bonnie Parker and Clyde Barrow, "Ma" Barker and her son Fred, "Pretty-Boy" Floyd, "Baby-Face" Nelson, and other dangerous criminals. In April 1936, FBI Director J. Edgar Hoover personally arrested Alvin Karpis as the "Public Enemy Number One" entered his car on a New Orleans street. Karpis, a leader of a gang whose members had killed ten people and stolen about a million dollars, had vowed to get Hoover after the Feds had gunned down his partners, the Barkers. Three years later, the infamous "Lepke" Buchalter, whose gang had extorted millions from small shopkeepers, surrendered to Director Hoover on a windy street corner in downtown New York.

The G-men were heroes. Kids bought G-man kits with badges, pistols, fingerprint pads, and holsters. Hundreds of thousands of tourists flocked to FBI headquarters in Washington to see the eyeglasses Dillinger wore when he was gunned down and other mementos of grisly deeds. There were magazine stories about G-men and movies portraying the clean-cut, brave, incorruptible men—far different from the ordinary cop —who brought the worst criminals to justice.

Over the years, triumph followed triumph. The FBI captured saboteurs landed on Long Island from a Nazi submarine. It tracked down fiends who blew up airliners to collect insurance, and captured Soviet master spy Rudolf Abel.

★ 5

The FBI became a true federal police force in the early 1930s when a series of laws authorized it to fight various interstate crimes and its agents to carry firearms and make arrests. Here, Director J. Edgar Hoover (*standing at right*) looks over President Franklin Roosevelt's shoulder as he signs a bill authorizing the bureau to track down robbers of national banks. The man standing beside Hoover is Secretary of the Treasury Henry Morgenthau, Jr.

(*United Press International*)

The image of relentless FBI agents spreading fear among hoodlums, serving justice and decency, has been carefully built up by the FBI, which has worked closely with authors and moviemakers. It has been perpetuated on television by Ephrem Zimbalist, Jr., Inspector Lew Erskine on television's popular show "The FBI."

The CIA, the Central Intelligence Agency, has been less successful in promoting popular legends about itself. It does not openly seek publicity, but its officials have encouraged friendly journalists and ex-agents to write about the agency in terms that give a limited and often inaccurate picture of what it really does. On the other hand, what it really does must often be kept secret. Most of our images of secret agents are based on such fictional characters as James Bond, agent 007 of the British Intelligence Service, MI 6. We see him surfacing in a cove on a Caribbean island, removing wet suit and scuba gear to blow up an oil storage tank. He has all sorts of thrilling adventures. He breaks into a castle, assassinates a mysterious figure, a woman who turns out to be a man expert in karate, and flees with the help of rockets strapped to his back.

We all have a trace of James Bond or Inspector Erskine in us. We would all like to go on secret missions, known as *covert operations* in CIA language. We would all like to be mysterious, with a shirt marked "S" for Superman hidden beneath our regular clothes.

We think of our secret agents, whether working at home or abroad, as heroes and those they play their tricks on as villains.

We applaud whatever our heroes do and look down on whatever the villains do, even if their acts are the same. A kidnapping by one of the good guys meets with our approval. When one of the bad guys kidnaps someone, we can't wait for him to be caught.

Such simple standards are all right in movies and television shows, where it is always made clear who the good guys are. In real life, it often is very difficult to know who the villains are, and they can often be detected only after a lot of careful digging for facts.

Long experience has taught us that no man is wise enough to take the law into his own hands and that unless there are rules that restrain government agents, the innocent will suffer along with the guilty. It was, in fact, this lesson that forged our nation.

Turn the clock back two hundred years to February 1761. At the bar in the Old State House in Boston was a case growing out of a controversy between the merchants of Boston and the king's officers. An act passed by Parliament a century before had created long-term search warrants that empowered their holders to enter any place to look for contraband goods. An officer possessing one of these "writs of assistance," as they were called, could go into any home, warehouse, office, building, or ship whether or not he had reason to suspect any smuggled goods were there, and he could in his search break locks, rifle cupboards, or even tear down walls and ceilings.

The writs were good from the time they were issued until six months after the death of the king reigning at the time. In 1760, King George II died, and the customs men in Boston had to apply for new writs good during the reign of George III. The Boston merchants, who hated the writs, seized on this as a chance to challenge the right of the Massachusetts governor to issue such papers and hired the noted attorney James Otis to represent them.

In his argument, Otis pointed out how these writs differed from ordinary search warrants that protected the "freedom of one's house." Ordinary warrants were sworn to by an officer who had to give his reasons for the search and also had to state exactly what he expected to find. They were valid only for a single search and had to be returned to the court that issued them by a certain date so that they could not be used again. The writs, on the other hand, opened every person's home and buildings to search. "Customs house officers may enter our houses as they please—we are commanded to permit their entry—their menial servants may enter—may break locks, bars and everything in their way—and whether they break through malice or revenge, no man, no court can inquire— bare suspicion without oath is sufficient." He told how one holder of a writ had revenged himself on a judge by forcing him to endure a search of his house from garret to cellar.

Otis lost the case and the governor of Massachusetts continued issuing the writs, but, as John Adams wrote, the "child Independence was born" in that courtroom when Otis asserted that the "freedom of one's house" was a right that stood above any law of Parliament.

It was precisely because Americans would not accept the fact that the government—the Parliament of England—could do whatever it liked that they broke with England. The limitation of the power of government was the issue on which the American Revolution was fought. The principle is enshrined in our Constitution.

As victims of tyranny, Americans of the revolutionary era were experts on the subject. They forbade their new government a whole list of practices that they knew, from experience, destroyed liberty:

Many Americans, or their forebears, had fled England to escape flogging and jailing without jury trial. They had been punished without being advised of their offense and tried without anyone to defend them or the chance to bring witnesses on their behalf. So the new government could not deprive anyone of "life, liberty or property, without due process of law" and was compelled to try all criminals speedily before an impartial jury.

They had been punished by special acts of Parliament directed at them; so such special laws, known as Bills of Attainder, were forbidden the new American government.

They had been tortured in the secret court of the Star

Chamber to make them confess crimes they had not committed. The new government was forbidden to force anyone to testify against himself.

They had been jailed for speaking out against offenses or for attending religious meetings, and so the Congress of the new government could not make any "law respecting the establishment of religion, or prohibiting the free exercise thereof; or abridging the freedom of speech, or of the press; or the right of the people peaceably to assemble, and to petition the Government for a redress of grievances."

Most of these rights were guaranteed either in the body of the Constitution or in its first ten amendments, also known as the Bill of Rights. The particular principle that Otis fought for in 1761 is enshrined in the fourth of these amendments entitled the Right of Search and Seizure Regulated: "The right of the people to be secure in their persons, houses, papers and effects against unreasonable searches and seizures, shall not be violated, and no warrants shall issue, but upon probable cause, supported by oath or affirmation, and particularly describing the place to be searched, and the persons or things to be seized."

The United States differs from every other nation on earth in that its government is strictly limited to those powers given it by the people. It is limited not just by promises—which many other governments have made to their people—but by independent courts and a system of laws that gives the individual the means to defend himself against oppression. Elsewhere, and throughout history, people have been the servants of their governments. In the United States the government is the servant of the people. It must obey rules.

There have been many changes in the two centuries since the birth of the "child Independence." A struggling nation of three million seaboard farmers, merchants, slave plantations, hunters, and craftsmen in a world of wood and leather has become a continental power with a population of 210 million, in a universe of electricity and uranium.

In many ways, the promise of our Declaration of Independence has been fulfilled. Liberty has been extended. In 1776, a third of our people were either slaves or indentured servants, with no liberty at all. In 1865, slavery was outlawed, and except for a few cases of peonage that crop up from time to time, all forms of involuntary servitude have been abolished. The Fourteenth Amendment, passed in 1868, made it necessary that all state laws conform to the rights guaranteed by the Constitution. This began a slow process that, in recent years, has brought an enormous increase in equality of rights to the poor and oppressed.

But the progress of liberty has not been steady, and contrary forces have always been at work. This conflict began even in the years of revolution, when the Continental Congress found it could not prosecute the war without using some of the same powers that, in British hands, it had found oppressive.

Can power exist and not be oppressive? The Congress did everything it could to control its use of power. It rationed it, giving it out in small portions hedged with restrictions. George Washington was commissioned to command the army, but could not even request a blanket without explaining why it was needed. The members of committees watched one another, and Congress watched the committees. On desperate occasions, the restrictions had to be lowered. Washington was given power to extend enlistments. This opened up the danger that he would build a personal army that could be used against Congress. But if he had not been given the power, there would have been no army at all. Either course was hazardous. Too little power was as dangerous as too much. Would the United States lose the war with bumbling committees or win it with a leader who would prove as odious as the British authority that had brought them to rebellion?

Power and liberty. Congress would strive to reconcile them through the somber years of revolution. Power and liberty are the warp and woof of American history. They are the two poles that make the dynamo spin. In 1861, seventy-eight years after the end of the Revolution, President Abraham Lincoln would ask: "Must a government, of necessity, be too strong for the liberties of its own people or too weak to maintain its own existence?"

This is the central riddle of our civilization. It cannot go away. It is basic to the very idea of free government and returns to trouble each generation of Americans in a different form.

One form in which it confronts us today is in the power wielded by two instruments of the government: the FBI and the CIA. Created for different reasons, both organizations have shown similar patterns of behavior.

In both cases, they were formed amid congressional doubts concerning their potential for abuse of liberty. In both cases, assurances were made that these abuses would not occur, and in both cases, the organizations developed in ways that confirmed the fears of those who presided over their birth.

The FBI was formed in 1908 as a special detective force in the Department of Justice. The CIA was formed in 1947 as a new agency to provide the government with information on the purposes and capabilities of other nations.

In 1907, during hearings on the need for a Justice Department Bureau of Investigation, Congressman J. Swager Sherley of Kentucky asserted that if our civilization stood for anything, it was "for a government where the humblest citizen is safeguarded against the secret activities of the executive of the government."

In 1973, there was only mild public surprise when, after a sixteen-year-old high school student sent a letter to the Socialist Workers party as part of a social studies assignment, her entire family was investigated by the FBI.

In 1947, during hearings on the need for a Central Intelligence Agency, Representative Henderson Lanham of Georgia expressed fears that the CIA might become like the Gestapo—the secret police that operated in Nazi Germany.

In 1975, the director of the agency admitted that it had been snooping on many American citizens including at least one member of Congress, in direct violation of its legal charter.

These agencies have broken the law. They have violated constitutional safeguards of our freedom. The FBI has in the past behaved like a lawless mob. It has provoked crimes, made it difficult for criminals to reform, persecuted political activists, and entangled innocent people in the snares of the law. The CIA has created enemies, corrupted young Americans, and built a dangerous distrust between the American people and their leaders, as we shall see in the following chapters.

The FBI and the CIA are not by any means the only agencies that have acted in an unconstitutional manner. More than a dozen other federal agencies possess police powers, and in recent years one after another has been discovered in lawless activities. Some examples: federal narcotics agents have raided the homes of innocent people; the Secret Service has spied on a presidential candidate; the Internal Revenue Service has spied on many civil rights, New Left, and other groups; U.S. Army Intelligence has spied on American civilians at home and abroad.

This book focuses on the FBI and the CIA because what they do touches the daily lives of more Americans to a greater extent than any of the other instruments of presidential power. Called into being to protect our country, both agencies must be watched carefully. Like powerful drugs, they can harm the patient along with the disease they combat. Whatever good they do, they can also be dangerous to our form of government. So dangerous, in fact, that the question arises, Can American democracy tolerate them?

In my reading of history I recall no instance where a government perished because of the absence of a secret-service force, but many there are that perished as a result of a spy system.

— J. SWAGER SHERLEY, Kentucky congressman, 1908

The Birth of the FBI

The FBI was formed in 1908, as a special detective force in the Department of Justice. It was not the first federal detective force. The first such group had been formed long before, during the Civil War, to track down counterfeiters of Greenbacks, the first paper money ever issued by the government. This force, known as the Secret Service, soon branched out into working on other Treasury Department cases, such as moonshining (selling whiskey without paying the federal whiskey tax). Another detective force was set up in the Post Office Department to deal with mail frauds and related crimes.

Other federal departments had less need for detectives. When they did need them, they borrowed them from the Secret Service. This was the situation when, in 1907, President Theodore Roosevelt's Attorney General, a flamboyant relative of Napoleon named Charles Joseph Bonaparte, asked Congress for money to set up his own detective force.

When Bonaparte told the members of the House Appropriations Committee how he and other departments were borrowing Secret Service men, the congressmen not only refused to give him money for his own detectives, but they also passed a law forbidding the Justice Department to use the Secret Service. They feared it was becoming some sort of central federal police force.

Attorney General Bonaparte's answer to fears that his men would be spying on citizens was that anyone could watch him as much as he pleased since he had nothing to hide. Besides, he assured the congressmen, agents would be prevented from abusing their powers by a tight system of control in which the Attorney General himself would receive daily reports on all their activities.

Congress passed the law forbidding Bonaparte to borrow any more Secret Service men on May 27, 1908, and adjourned three days later. A month later, Bonaparte appointed some Justice Department agents on his own, in a newly formed Bureau of Investigation. (It took the name Federal Bureau of Investigation [FBI] in 1935.)

The reason Bonaparte needed detectives, and the reason his predecessors for some thirty years had been borrowing Secret Service men, lay in the growing responsibilities of the federal government. Earlier heads of the Justice Department had not needed detectives because they could use local police forces or marshals, appointed by the courts, to enforce the few laws that state or local police could not handle. But new laws were passed. The enforcement of some of these laws required special detective work. Others represented the extension of the federal government into new areas.

The attorneys general needed detectives to run down violations of the antitrust laws passed in 1890 and also to help solve crimes that crossed state lines with increasing frequency as speedy railroads crisscrossed the nation.

Whatever Bonaparte's justification, he faced a battle when he went back to Congress the following year for funds to pay for his agents. Congress was still against the idea, but President Roosevelt came to his aid in a public campaign in which he pictured the legislators as helping criminals by refusing funds that would lead to their capture. Congress caved in and Bonaparte got his money.

Organizations take on a life of their own, and the FBI was no exception. The staff of the bureau wanted to make certain it continued to get money from Congress, and it wanted to expand.

In 1910, Congress passed the Mann Act, a foolish law that forbade the carrying of women across state lines for immoral purposes. It was aimed at prostitution, heretofore always regarded as strictly a local police matter; but the law was so loosely worded that it actually made it criminal for a man to take his girl friend to another state even if she was willing or suggested the trip.

The Bureau seized upon this law to make itself more important. Its chief, Stanley Finch, began telling Congress how every female in the nation was threatened by rings of "white slavers" out to force them into lives of degradation. "Unless a girl was actually confined to a room and guarded," he said, "there was no girl, regardless of her status in life, who was altogether safe." This included, of course, wives, daughters, and mothers of congressmen. The painting of dire threats that could only be quelled by the FBI was a method that would be used over and again to wrest money from Congress.

To "protect" America's wives and mothers, FBI agents went all over the country inspecting whorehouses and making censuses of their inhabitants so they could keep track of arrivals and departures. They also hired madams and tarts as informers and tapped telephones to learn of assignations for illegal interstate embraces. It was in the enforcement of the Mann Act that large-scale prying into the private affairs of citizens began, in a manner that would have been resented by those who fought the American Revolution.

If bureau agents were prepared to watch private citizens entering brothels and escorting their girl friends by Pullman car, what would they do if Attorney General Palmer asked them to protect the nation against revolution? When it comes to maintaining the nation, as we have seen, even President Lincoln was puzzled as to how far he could go without so violating the Constitution that its spirit would be destroyed.

If a suspicion that aliens are dangerous constitutes the justification of that power exercised over them by Congress, then a similar suspicion will justify the exercise of a similar power over natives.

—JAMES MADISON, January 23, 1799

When the Reds Were Rounded Up

It is a little after eleven o'clock, Sunday night, June 2, 1919, on a quiet residential street in Washington, D.C. The Attorney General of the United States, a Pennsylvania Quaker named A. Mitchell Palmer, is on the second floor of his spacious home, preparing for bed.

Suddenly there is a thump at the front door. An explosion shakes the entire building, followed by the tinkling of shattered windows. The occupant of the house across the street, Assistant Secretary of the Navy Franklin Roosevelt, rushes out his front door to find a fragment of a body. Another piece of flesh has blown through an open window of the nearby house of the Norwegian ambassador.

That same night, bombs exploded in New York City; Cleveland; Newtonville, Massachusetts; Paterson, New Jersey; Boston; Pittsburgh; and Philadelphia. The targets were judges, prominent businessmen, a mayor, a legislator, and a police inspector.

The only casualties were a night watchman at the home of General Sessions Judge Charles C. Nott, Jr., in New York, and the bomber of the Attorney General's home, whose body fragments were found up and down R Street, N.W., in Washington.

Pink handbills, at the sites of most of the bombings, were signed by THE ANARCHIST FIGHTERS, who announced that they intended to kill and destroy those in America who opposed the "worldwide spread of revolution."

A month earlier, on the eve of May Day, the international workers' holiday, another bomb had injured two people in the home of Senator Thomas Hardwick of Georgia. An attempt had also been made to destroy the home of the mayor of Seattle, and sixteen other bombs, addressed to prominent citizens, had been found in the New York City Post Office. (They had not been delivered because of insufficient postage.)

The country was in an unsettled state. The First World War had ended just seven months before. One of the Allies, Russia, was in the hands of the Bolsheviks, and communists had seized power in Hungary and were threatening to take over Germany. In the United States there were plenty of signs of unrest. Inflation had halved the value of the dollar while most wages had not kept pace. Many people found themselves worse off than they had ever been before.

The end of war spending forced plants to cut back work forces. Unemployment grew, strikes were threatened, and radical labor leaders urged workers to band together against the capitalists who owned the factories.

In this atmosphere, the bombs were widely taken as a sign that revolution was imminent in the United States. Attorney General Palmer did nothing to discourage this idea, and a hysterical Congress voted him $500,000 to save the country.

Neither the Attorney General nor anyone else knew who had planted the explosives, but Palmer declared that the "reds" were responsible. What should have been an investigation aimed at criminal bomb-throwers became a crusade aimed at rooting out all who thought in violent terms, whether they actually made bombs or not. The method was like trying to solve a case of arson by rounding up everyone with matches.

Palmer perceived his main target to be communists, even though the Communist party in the United States, as such, didn't exist at the time of the bombings. It was born at the beginning of September, three months after the June bombs, out of a split in the Socialist party.

The American Socialist party, which had long been growing in strength and had won 6 percent of the votes in the 1916 presidential election, had become unpopular because of its outright opposition to World War I. Many of its leaders had been jailed for fighting the draft and preaching pacifism. Then, after the most radical Russian socialists, the Bolsheviks, seized power, the weakened American Socialist party was increasingly divided. Those socialists who continued to adhere to the traditional democratic belief that they must strive for approval of the voters in free elections retained control of the organization. The others, who believed that violent revolution was necessary to bring about socialism, left the party or were expelled. They formed the Communist party. The communists were feared not only because they preached revolution, but because it was suspected that they received help from the Soviet Bolsheviks.

This was later shown to be true; but in 1919, with the newly formed Soviet government fighting for its life, there was no reason to fear American communists as a particular threat to the United States.

Attorney General Palmer didn't see it this way. He put a new man in charge of the bureau, giving him a free hand "to deal with the situation . . . in his own way." He also named

★ **20**

a new Assistant Attorney General to take charge of investigations and prosecutions of radicals and set up a new Justice Department division to study subversive activities.

The new head of the bureau was William J. Flynn, former head of the Treasury Department's Secret Service. In charge of the new General Intelligence Division (GID) was a twenty-four-year-old department law clerk who had been working on alien registration. His name was J. Edgar Hoover. Hoover, who had once been a card indexer at the Library of Congress, began organizing a file system on American radicals that soon held more than 200,000 names. By November, his GID staff had prepared biographies of 60,000 of their leaders. Almost half of the 400 special agents in the bureau were assigned to the hunt for subversives. Many were successful in infiltrating their ranks, some posing as wild agitators. By December 1919, a federal judge was to note that FBI men had become "an active and efficient part of the Communist Party."

All that summer, while Hoover's men were compiling their dossiers, the President of the United States, Woodrow Wilson, was involved in a bitter battle with the Senate. President Wilson was trying to get the Senate to agree that the United States should join the League of Nations. That September, while taking to the people his argument that U.S. membership in the League was necessary to prevent future wars, the President suffered a stroke. He was thereafter incapable of exercising the powers of his office, and the nation remained leaderless.

July, August, and September had passed, and the bomb plotters remained uncaptured. Newspapers cried out for blood, and the Senate passed a resolution urging Attorney General Palmer to get on with his task.

Finally, on the night of Thursday, November 7, the bureau agents struck. In twelve cities, a series of raids against members of the Federation of the Union of Russian Workers resulted in more than a thousand arrests and the deportation of 249 aliens to Russia. The federation, a little-known organization founded a dozen years before, boasted that it was made up of atheists, communists, and anarchists. Even though none of its members was connected with any bombs and no weapons were found, the Attorney General was widely acclaimed as a hero. A week after the raid, Palmer reported to the Senate that radicals were close to taking over the country. Despite its approval of Palmer's actions, the Senate refused his request for a law that would make it a crime for anyone to preach revolution, whether the words were accompanied by actions or not.

British journalist Alfred George Gardiner, who was visiting the country in the fall of 1919, remarked on "the feverish condition of the public mind . . . hag-ridden by the spectre of Bolshevism . . . the horrid name 'Radical' covered the most innocent departure from conventional thought. 'America,' as a wit of the time said, 'is the land of liberty—liberty to keep in step.' "

This was the atmosphere of the country as it reached the new year.

Two days later, on January 2, 1920, at nine in the evening, some members of the Communist party were sitting in a back room of the party's Boston headquarters waiting for others to arrive for a meeting. The back and front doors were suddenly thrown open and men, wearing ordinary street clothes, rushed in with guns in their hands. Twenty-seven members were rounded up, herded against a wall, and searched. Then they were marched downstairs to the street, where they saw waiting for them rows of Boston cops. They were put into vans and taken to a police station.

Each of the members was questioned at the police station by an agent of the Bureau of Investigation. He had to state whether he was a citizen and whether he was a member of the Communist party and was asked to describe his party activities.

What happened to one of the arrested communists was

given in testimony at a later federal trial. The witness, Henry
G. Steiner, was a thirty-five-year-old clerk who had been born
in Manchester, New Hampshire. After being jailed for one day
without explanation, Steiner was released. Two days later, on
Monday night, a bureau agent came to his home to make a
search.

"I said to him," Steiner testified, " 'I don't know who you
are; have you any credentials or warrant?' He displayed his
badge and said that was all the warrant he required. . . . It
was a gilt badge and I think it said 'Department of Justice.'
. . . He then proceeded to search; that is, he did ask me where
I kept my books, literature of various kinds. I told him that
he would find everything right out in plain sight in the bookcase. He went to the bookcase and proceeded to search for
anything he thought he could use. He went to a table where I
had books and papers of various kinds and went through them.
He went up to another rack, another part of the room, and he
took what he wanted from that. He pulled open several draw-
ers, but he found they contained other than books or pamphlets, and he finally inquired if that was all I had. I said, 'You
will find everything that I have got right there.' "

The agent took Steiner and a lot of his books down to
the Boston offices of the Department of Justice. Steiner was
sent home, and a few days later everything that had been taken
from him was returned except for "certain papers."

Steiner was one of some 800 to 1,200 persons arrested
on the night of January 2 in Boston, Chelsea, Brockton, and
seventeen other cities in Massachusetts and New Hampshire.
He was one of some 10,000 arrested all over the country.
Many had been attending Communist party meetings that had
been held that night at the urging of bureau agents or their
informers working inside the party.

Of the 10,000, about 3,000 were imprisoned, some for
periods of several months. These included women separated
from their young children and many poor people whose jailing

★ 23

"Reds," rounded up in New York City on the night of January 2, 1920, are herded aboard ferries to be incarcerated—some for many weeks—on Ellis Island. *(United Press International)*

created financial hardship for their families. In Detroit, 800 people were kept for six days in a 448-square-foot corridor serviced by one toilet. Of those seized in Boston, 440 were put in unheated cells on Deer Island, where conditions were so bad that one prisoner killed himself by jumping from a fifth-floor window.

Some of those who were held did not even have a connection with anything radical. Thirty-nine men seized in Lynn, Massachusetts, for example, were found to have been organizing a cooperative bakery. Even Communist party members did not necessarily hold radical opinions. Some had joined various ethnic clubs for social reasons. The Ukrainian Socialist Club in Chicago, for example, attracted members because it offered the only authentic Ukrainian food in the city. Others joined to study English or arithmetic. Then, as members of Socialist party branches expelled by the party, they had automatically become communists in September 1919. If their leaders knew the revolutionary ideas that had forced them out of the Socialist party, the members often knew nothing more than that the name of their groups had been changed. And even when they were aware of their party's sympathy with the Bolsheviks, they often agreed with this more as former victims of czarist oppression than as enemies of America.

A minister of the Methodist Episcopal Church who visited the jails found that many of the prisoners were hardworking skilled or semiskilled laborers with small savings. They were typical immigrants, often with a poor command of English, struggling to make the most of their opportunities.

Prominent lawyers protested that the mass arrests and searches violated constitutional rights. As complaints mounted, investigations were held by both houses of Congress. It was during these hearings that the facts about the raids emerged.

Laws could have been applied against those who plotted the overthrow of the government by force, but the bureau agents had not acted under these laws because they lacked any evidence of revolution that would stand up in court. There was plenty of evidence of *talking* about revolution—books and pamphlets and conversations overheard by informers at meetings—but talk is not the same as action, or even as preparation for action. The Justice Department had lost a case in which it tried to get the courts to declare that talking about violence was as bad as violence itself.

Communist literature and speech was full of calls to class warfare and declarations that free elections were a fake, but no court could be found to say that such words were the same as actual rebellion. Even when a judge would agree that the purpose of the Communist party was the "capture and destruction of the State . . . by force and violence," he would add that there was no danger of this happening in the near future.

American communists who preached violence without doing anything directly about it, such as obtaining arms or explosives, were not breaking any law. Attorney General Palmer had asked Congress for legislation that would punish them for merely talking about revolution. When Congress refused, the only way he could get at the "reds" was to attack those who were not citizens. Aliens were subject to a special law that said they could be deported if they merely *belonged* to any group that preached violent overthrow of the government.

To take action under this law, Palmer had to work with the Labor Department, which administered the alien laws. The Labor Department, with only a small staff of immigration inspectors, tried to administer the law fairly. It looked into each case separately and gave each suspected alien a chance to defend himself. The Justice Department used the law as an excuse for mass arrests. Hundreds of FBI agents collected names of members of these groups and sent the names of those thought to be aliens to the Labor Department. The Labor Department made out arrest warrants, using the FBI agents' information, and sent the warrants to the FBI, which then used them to make arrests. The only other part played by the Labor Department was to have an inspector at a police station to watch while FBI agents grilled the suspects.

Some senators thought the raids were all right, on the ground that the Constitution did not apply to aliens and that the Attorney General was dealing with an emergency. But Senator Thomas Walsh of Montana, head of the Senate Committee that investigated the Justice Department, found that with few exceptions, aliens were protected by the Constitution. He spelled out all the ways in which the law had been broken.

First, the arrest warrants were illegal because the FBI agents had not sworn an oath to obtain them but had merely requested them from the Labor Department. This violated the Fourth Amendment, which says that "no warrant shall issue but upon probable cause, supported by oath or affirmation."

Second, many of those arrested did not have even these illegal warrants outstanding against them. The FBI agents had simply arrested everyone found on the premises. In Detroit, for example, this resulted in the detainment of a band that had been hired to play in the hall.

Third, many searches were made without search warrants. This violated the Fourth Amendment prohibition of "unreasonable searches and seizures."

Fourth, even when search warrants were obtained, there was no law that authorized searches in connection with the deportation of aliens.

There was also a serious question as to whether it was legal for the Justice Department or its agents to arrest persons on behalf of the Labor Department. It was also found that a Labor Department rule that extended to aliens the rights to consult an attorney and be advised of the charges against them had been suspended in January without the knowledge of the Secretary of Labor or of his assistant in charge of these matters.

In any event, the very idea of mass arrests was a mistake. Even where there had been actual armed revolt against the government, as in the Whisky Rebellion of 1794 and the Civil War, no mass arrests had been made. If, in real revolts, only leaders had been held, what possible excuse could there be for arresting everyone when there had been no revolt?

All this caused Federal Judge George W. Anderson in Boston to describe those "supposedly law-enforcing officials" who carried out the raids as a mob. "A mob is a mob," he remarked, "whether made up of government officials acting under instructions from the Department of Justice, or of criminals [and] loafers. . . ."

J. Edgar Hoover, who as head of the General Intelligence Division had played an important part in planning the raids, later disavowed them. In 1947, he told the New York *Herald Tribune* that he "deplored the manner in which the raids were executed then, and my position has remained unchanged."

How was it possible for law-enforcement officials of the Justice Department to become, in effect, a lawless mob?

There was an attorney general whose home and family had almost been destroyed by a terrorist's bomb.

There was the hysteria of a country emerging from the brutalizing influence of a war into a new world situation.

There was an absence of government leadership due to President Wilson's stroke.

And, finally, we must recognize that the existence of the FBI itself made possible actions that would have been undreamed of by former attorneys general. Whatever the hysterical demands of Congress and the press, the Attorney General would not have been able to carry out the raids had he not had at his disposal a force of several hundred agents willing to do his bidding.

In this way, lawless impulses became lawless actions, savoring, in the words of Secretary of State Charles Evans Hughes, "of the worst practices of tyranny." Precious constitutional guarantees, at the basis of this country's greatness, were suspended against those who needed them most—the weak and friendless.

Perhaps it is a universal truth that loss of liberty at home is to be charged to provisions against danger, real or pretended, from abroad.
— JAMES MADISON in the Viriginia Assembly, January 23, 1799

The Persecution of William Walter Remington

BACKGROUND

For some time after the Palmer raids, the FBI did not trouble itself with the political beliefs of other Americans. Mr. Palmer kept warning of the "red menace" much as Director Finch had warned that America's wives and mothers were in danger of being made into prostitutes, but nothing could keep communist-chasing from falling into disrepute.

J. Edgar Hoover, who as head of the GID had played a leading role in the raids, became head of the bureau in 1924. He quickly improved the training and standards of FBI agents, ridding the bureau of the scandal that had tainted it during the corrupt administration of President Harding (1920–23).

Menacing developments abroad put the FBI back in the business of political spying. In 1936, hostility was increasingly dividing the planet. Japan was expanding its empire in China,

★ 30

*Nazi Germany was rearming, the Italian Fascists were con-
quering Ethiopia, and right-wing Spaniards under General
Francisco Franco were waging civil war against their Republican government.*

*The Spanish Civil War marked a new phase of hostilities.
For with Germany and Italy supporting Franco and the Soviet
Union supporting the Loyalist government, different European
nations were opposing each other on the field of battle for the
first time in eighteen years.*

*In this atmosphere, President Franklin Roosevelt asked
Director Hoover to keep track of the efforts of agents of the
German, Italian, and Russian dictatorships who were seeking
support here. Since the agents would be recruiting Americans,
or supplying them with money, this task involved spying on
Americans, particularly members of groups like the German-
American Bund or the Communist party, whose policies sup-
ported foreign powers.*

*The interests of the Justice Department and the FBI in
communists waxed and waned with shifts in Communist party
policy and world events. In the ten-year period 1936–46, So-
viet-American relations changed three times with almost dizzy-
ing abruptness. In 1939, with the signing of the Hitler-Stalin
pact, the two nations shifted from coolness to enmity. The
German invasion of Russia in June 1941 marked a shift from
enmity to warm friendship as the two nations became wartime
allies. In 1946, the shift was back in the other direction, from
friendship to hostility as the cold war began.*

*By 1947, the United States was helping Greece and Tur-
key fight communist guerrillas. At home, President Truman
ordered the Civil Service Commission to check the loyalties of
all 2.3 million government employees. They were to be
screened not just for disloyal acts but for any indications that
they might possibly be disloyal. Disloyal acts, such as giving
information to enemies of the country, were illegal and could
be punished under the espionage laws. Possible disloyalty was*

something else. It meant that because of something a person had said, or the kinds of people he had known, there was a risk that he would become a traitor.

A finding that a person was a security risk was a serious matter. In some countries—Britain, for example—security risks were just quietly transferred to jobs in which they had no opportunity to harm the nation's interests. Under the Truman program, however, security risks were discharged from government service. They could fight for their jobs by appealing to a Loyalty Review Board, but their pay was cut off the moment they were dismissed. In other words, they were punished, and presumed guilty, until they could prove themselves innocent.

Measuring a person's disloyalty is a difficult task. It was made easier for the loyalty boards by methods that put the burden of proof on the accused. The loyalty boards received information on government workers from any source. An informer could remain anonymous, so that the accused had no chance of facing his accuser or even of finding out exactly what the charge against him was.

Constitutional protections were not used because it was thought that security measures came under the government's right to hire and discharge employees. A government job, according to this theory, was a privilege. (Years later, the Supreme Court disagreed with this and constitutional protections were extended to those involved in loyalty hearings.)

The FBI was asked to put its agents at the disposal of the Civil Service loyalty boards to carry out investigations where there was reason for suspecting an employee. To assist it in this task, the FBI once more had its voluminous files on individuals and organizations, files that it had been expanding since 1936.

Since our adversary in the cold war was the Soviet Union, the loyalty program was directed at finding employees who were more loyal to the USSR than to the United States. The *test used by the loyalty boards was membership in the Communist party or in "front" groups affiliated with it.*

With all the shifts in Soviet and American policy between 1936 and 1946, measuring loyalty by communist affiliation would have been difficult at best. But the conditions under which the loyalty boards operated were far from ideal. Unreasoning fear had gripped the country after World War I; now, after victory in another great conflict, a similar nervousness was abroad in the land.

There was a difference, though. In 1919, the United States had been safe against any conceivable threat. In 1947, new weapons—the atom bomb and long-range aircraft—indicated that the United States could no longer indefinitely count on the broad ocean barriers for protection. In these circumstances, the idea of "national security" began to take on a new, almost sacred meaning.

William Walter Remington had a bright future in government. At age thirty, he had an important job in the Commerce Department in the export division that made decisions regarding shipments of important materials to other countries.

He was a handsome, clean-cut fellow, more than six feet tall, with blond hair and blue eyes. He was making $10,300 a year, a high salary in government in 1948, especially for a man of his age. It had been eight years since he had first gone to work for the government. He had been in Washington since 1940, the year he got his master's degree from Columbia University. He was hard-working, ambitious, and respected by his colleagues.

His personal life was not so successful. He was separated from his wife, Ann, and his two small children. He lived alone in a small apartment. If he was lonely at times, his existence was also more peaceful than it had been. Things would get better. They always did.

If he could have looked ahead five years, to 1953, he

would probably have seen himself in a much higher position in the Commerce Department, perhaps on the way to becoming an economic adviser to the President, living in a comfortable house with a new wife and family.

The reality would be different. In 1953, he would be in Lewisburg Prison. In 1954, he would be dead.

His ruin began in May 1948. One day he learned that his loyalty was being investigated. Friends told him that FBI men were asking questions about him. Remington had an idea of what the investigation was about, but he couldn't take it seriously.

A year before, three polite FBI agents had called on him and showed him a photograph of a lady they said was Elizabeth Bentley. Remington had recognized the face, but he had told them that he had known the lady as "Helen Johnson." He had told the agents a great deal about himself and about how he had met "Helen Johnson."

Born in 1918, in Ridgewood, New Jersey, Remington had come of age during the Great Depression of the 1930s. His father, an insurance supervisor, hard-pressed then like most people, had just managed to send him to Dartmouth College in New Hampshire, in 1934. Bill Remington was very bright, entering college at sixteen. He was also outspoken and politically radical.

He argued with everyone and said whatever he thought. A conservative classmate thought he was a communist. The campus communists wanted no part of him because he made them look foolish in arguments and wouldn't let anyone do his thinking for him. He took a year off, 1936–37, to earn enough money to finish his education, working as a messenger for the Tennessee Valley Authority in Knoxville. He graduated in 1938, at the top of his class.

That same year he met a pretty Bennington College senior named Ann Moos. Ann's views were to the left of his own, and Ann's mother's views were even further to the left. When he married Ann that summer, he acquired a mother-in-law who was a communist.

During the years 1938–40, while Remington was taking his master's degree at Columbia University in New York City, he and Ann were frequent weekend visitors at Ann's mother's spacious house in Croton, New York. Many of the other guests were communists.

Remington and his wife had sympathized with the Spanish Loyalists and given money to help them. But the Hitler-Stalin pact and the Russian invasion of Finland put them at loggerheads with Ann's mother, Mrs. Elizabeth Moos, and her friends, moving the Remingtons out of sympathy with communism. They still visited Mrs. Moos, however, even after they moved to Washington in 1940, when William was hired by the National Resources Planning Board. Remington was working for the War Production Board in March 1942, when Joe North, a communist editor he and his wife had met in Croton, introduced him to "Helen Johnson" and "John" Golos.

North said that Golos was writing a book about war production and that the dark-haired "Helen Johnson" was his research assistant. Golos explained that "Helen" also did research for reporters for the newspaper *PM* and other publications, and he asked if she might call on Remington once in a while for information. Remington agreed.

After telling the FBI all about Ann Moos and her mother and about his meeting with Golos and "Helen Johnson," Remington had continued sending the bureau information on communists who were attempting to take over a veterans group he belonged to, and had notified bureau agents of attempts by some other friends of Joe North to contact him. "I am just as eager as you are to help rid this country of communists and their sympathizers," he wrote to Special Agent Cornelison of the FBI's Washington field office.

Elizabeth Bentley, whose stories had caused the FBI to question Remington in 1947, had told the FBI that from 1940 to 1945, as "Helen Johnson" or "Helen Grant," she had worked as a messenger getting information from American government officials to be sent to the Soviet Union. The person who transmitted the information was Jacob Golos, who posed as a travel agent. She named about thirty government officials who, she alleged, had given her secret information. Remington she had described as the least important, a "minor figure" who had not known that the information he gave her would go to the Soviet Union.

As the cold war became more intense, more and more people were getting worried about communist infiltration of the government. Passing secrets to the Soviets while they were wartime allies did not seem a very serious matter in 1945 when Miss Bentley first told her story. But in 1947, with the communists tightening their hold over Poland and other countries of Eastern Europe and gaining strength in Italy and France, and with leftist guerrillas fighting in Greece, those who would help the Soviets from inside the U.S. government appeared more menacing. For this reason, in April 1947, a federal grand jury in New York began investigating Miss Bentley's charges.

The grand jury did not accomplish much. As the law was then, a person could be convicted of espionage only if indicted within three years of committing the crime. By April 1947, indictments could be brought only against persons who had passed secrets after April 1944, during the last year and a half of Miss Bentley's courier activities. In any event, no charges were made against any of the people she had named.

In the spring of 1948, Czechoslovakia was taken over by the communists, and Foreign Minister Jan Masaryk, who had many friends in the United States, killed himself. All through that year, the Chinese communists continued advancing against the U.S.-backed Nationalists in an enormous civil war. Some Americans had such belief in the strength of their country that they could not believe that anything could happen anywhere in the world without its help. From this assumption

★ **36**

it followed that the United States, in some way, was helping the communists. Fanatics believed that Presidents Roosevelt and Truman were somehow in league with the sinister Russian dictator, Stalin. Those somewhat less extreme thought that if the two Presidents were not actively helping Stalin, they at least had been deceived by traitors within the government.

There were, therefore, in 1948, three different currents of opinion all bearing on the problem of loyalty of government employees. First, there were the fanatics, who blamed all communist advances on traitors and suspected an evil or stupid government of protecting them. Second, as the 1948 presidential election approached, Republican politicians saw that any evidence of treason during the Roosevelt and Truman administrations could be used to discredit the Democrats and help the Republicans win the White House. Since the Republicans had gained control of both houses of Congress in the 1946 elections, they could use congressional committees to promote this view. Third, some were genuinely concerned that persons who had passed secrets to the Russians between 1941 and 1945 might still be in a position to do so in 1948.

These three groups had different ways of looking at the government loyalty program. The first group, convinced that the government was plotting with the communists, regarded the loyalty program as a fake. The second, eager to make political capital out of any evidence of treason, feared that the loyalty program would succeed. (If it did quietly rid the government of traitors, they would not be able to make an issue out of the Democrats' tolerance of communists in government.) The third group wanted the loyalty program to succeed.

Into this whirlpool of conflicting desires came a sensational series of newspaper articles based on Miss Bentley's experiences as a "Soviet spy queen." She was called before committees of the Senate and House to testify.

The committees were especially interested in hearing about Remington. Of the thirty people Miss Bentley had

★ 37

named, Remington was almost the only one still in government service. In order to show that the government loyalty program was a failure, the Senate subcommittee needed to attack someone who was still employed. And it had to do it right away, before the government's loyalty investigation of Remington, which had been under way for two months, was completed.

As the head of the House Committee on Un-American Activities, Congressman J. Parnell Thomas, later explained it, he and his Republican colleagues wanted to "keep the heat on Harry Truman."

Miss Bentley and Remington, who immediately became famous as a result of their televised appearances before the Senate subcommittee, told two different stories.

Miss Bentley said that Remington had given her government secrets in 1942 and 1943 while he was working for the War Production Board. She added that he was a communist, who had paid party dues through her.

Remington admitted giving Miss Bentley information which, he said, was simply in the nature of checking or confirming stories that she showed him in two newspapers, *PM* and the communist *Daily Worker,* information she had said she needed as a research assistant to reporters on the papers. He denied knowing that Miss Bentley was a spy, and he also denied that he had ever been a member of the Communist party. Any money he had given her, he said, was a contribution to a fund for Spanish Loyalist veterans.

Meanwhile, the official government loyalty check, which the Senate subcommittee was attacking, was proceeding. President Truman's orders concerning loyalty had made clear that this meant loyalty in recent years. Past interests, enthusiasms, and affiliations, particularly those going back to years before a person was employed by the government, were not to be taken as signs of present disloyalty. The loyalty boards were supposed to take into account that people learned and matured. Their investigations were supposed to be directed at

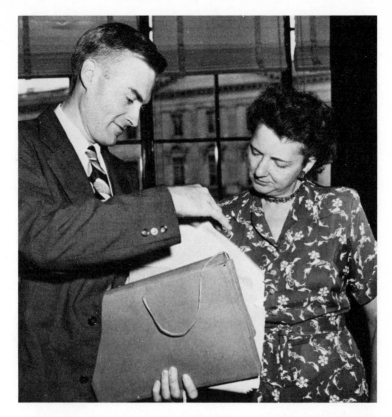

William Remington confers with Elizabeth Bentley on August 2, 1948, the day he testified before the Senate subcommittee. At this point, Remington still thought that the "spy queen" had just made a mistake when she called him communist.　　　　　　　(*United Press International*)

determining the present character and loyalty of those who worked for the government. Justice Hugo Black's previous membership in the Ku Klux Klan while a young attorney in Alabama had proved irrelevant to his distinguished career on the Supreme Court.

On September 20, 1948, the four men and one woman of the loyalty board of the Fourth Civil Service Region found Remington a loyalty risk and ordered him suspended from government service. Remington appealed the matter to the Loyalty Review Board, and his appeal was successful. Remington was reinstated and given the pay owing to him for the period he had been suspended.

Miss Bentley, twice invited by the review board to appear,

★ 39

had twice declined; she then told a newspaper reporter she had never been asked. She had also, on September 12, repeated her charge against Remington on the "Meet the Press" show on NBC television. A statement made on television is not protected as is testimony before a congressional committee, and Remington sued for libel when she did not make a retraction. He won the libel suit when NBC and the show's sponsor settled out of court for $9,000.

The matter would now seem to have been settled once and for all. William Remington had been validated by the Loyalty Review Board and a libel suit. Miss Bentley had been discredited.

Her position was difficult. She had named a lot of names and made a lot of accusations. It is possible that some of them were true, but nothing she said had been confirmed, except by other former communists. Not a single one of the thirty persons she had named had been indicted for any crime, and the ten she had said were ringleaders had refused to testify when subpoenaed by the House committee.

As far as the legal evidence went, there was nothing to support any of Miss Bentley's accusations. In the one case that had gone to court, she had been made to look like a liar.

As things were in those days, this could not be allowed to stand, especially with the Democrats back in the White House after President Truman's surprising 1948 election victory. Elizabeth Bentley's credibility was important to too many people. Not just to Republican politicians, but to all the professional anticommunists who were making a living writing and lecturing to others about the communist menace—and to the FBI, which had been promoting the lady as living proof of the menace they were being paid to combat.

With Remington remaining in a high government post, cleared of disloyalty, and Miss Bentley's accusations costing a television station and sponsor $9,000, it would become more and more difficult to get more newspaper headlines about government traitors. Who would believe any charges made in congressional committee hearings if they were shown to be based on the careless statements of an irresponsible woman? If the image of Elizabeth Bentley as an authentic "spy queen" was to be rebuilt, Remington would have to be destroyed.

The process of destroying Remington took three years, two grand juries, and two trials. During this time, the FBI expended a great deal of fruitless effort to find witnesses to prove that Remington had been a member of the Communist party.

It took a third grand jury, and an illegal inquisition of Ann Remington, to produce an indictment. Mrs. Remington had not been called earlier because, as his wife, she could not testify against him. Now, however, they were divorced.

The new grand jury was able to extract from Mrs. Remington corroboration of Miss Bentley's stories. This was obtained from Ann Remington by methods so unfair that Judge Learned Hand of the federal Court of Appeals was to describe the case as one of the most dreadful miscarriages of justice he had witnessed in his long career.

There were many unusual features of this third grand jury proceeding. Thomas E. Donegan, the federal prosecutor, a former FBI man, had served as Miss Bentley's personal attorney several years before. The foreman of the grand jury, John Brunini, was a *partner* and *collaborator* of Miss Bentley's in connection with a book she was writing for Devin-Adair Publishing Company. Thus, the head of the jury certainly, and the prosecutor possibly, had a personal interest in seeing that Miss Bentley's truthfulness was re-established. As Judge Learned Hand showed in his opinion on the case, Donegan and Brunini worked together to force from Mrs. Remington, by illegal and third-degree methods, admissions damaging to her former husband.

Brunini deceived Mrs. Remington in telling her that she could not withhold any information on the grounds that it was something she could have known only as Remington's former wife. Then Brunini told her that if she refused on these grounds (which she really had a right to do), she could be put in jail until she agreed to answer and that if she did not answer correctly, she could be imprisoned for perjury (lying under oath).

Thus she was put in the position of believing that she had to answer a question and that if she did not give the "right" answer she would go to jail. Had a judge been present, he would have corrected this false impression. Donegan, who, as an attorney, knew Brunini was giving Mrs. Remington incorrect legal advice, had stood by and remained silent.

For hours, Brunini and Donegan hammered away at Ann Remington to answer whether some money Remington had given Miss Bentley was for the Communist party. This was a tricky question. Remington had admitted the money was to help the Spanish Loyalists, but since many groups that helped the Loyalists were dominated by communists, and since Remington could very well have suspected that Miss Bentley was a communist, he could have known that his contribution was to be passed on to the Loyalists by a communist group. There was no reason for him to see anything wrong in this at the time it happened, nor was this at all the same as paying dues to the Communist party.

No doubt Ann Remington was aware of this. When she was asked, "All you have to do is say yes or no as to whether that money was for the Communist party," she refused to answer. This was her only safe course. If she said yes, she feared this would be understood as saying her former husband was a communist. If she said no, she could be threatened with perjury on the grounds that whatever group got the money was a Communist party front.

Having on false grounds convinced Ann Remington that she had to answer yes or no, Brunini and Donegan forced her to choose between helping them or being jailed for perjury. She chose to help them. Once she had crossed that line, she gave them the answers they wanted. She told them that Remington had been a communist at Dartmouth. (She had not known him then and this contradicted testimony of people who *had* known him there, including the president and dean of the college.) She also testified that she had seen her husband pass secret information to Miss Bentley, even though the "spy queen" had claimed all along that she and Remington had always been alone when he gave her information.

Everything Ann Remington told the grand jury, she later repeated in court at her former husband's trial, fearing that any change of her grand jury testimony would leave her open to perjury charges.

Armed with Ann Remington's admissions, Donegan haled Remington before the grand jury and asked him if he had ever been a communist. When he said he had not, he was indicted for perjury. On the day of the indictment, June 8, 1950, he was dismissed from his Commerce Department job not for disloyalty, but "in the interests of good administration."

The FBI continued its efforts to find other witnesses to Remington's membership in the Communist party. It went so far as to take one former communist from Massachusetts to Knoxville to refresh his memory for places and people. Despite such efforts, it was unable to produce a single witness whose testimony would stand up in court. It was more successful in keeping out of the courtroom witnesses who could have proved that Remington was not a communist.

Remington's attorney, William C. Chanler, had found two former New Hampshire communists who agreed to come to New York and testify that Remington had never been a member of the party. (Dartmouth College is in New Hampshire.) Chanler also found the lady who kept the Communist party's records in New Hampshire. She told Chanler that she would testify that Remington's name had never been on the party's rolls. The lawyer telephoned the New Hampshire witnesses from his New York office, but when they arrived in New

York the next morning, two FBI agents, who must have been notified by means of wiretaps on the telephones in Chanler's office, were waiting on the station platform with subpoenas for them to appear before the grand jury, which was kept sitting throughout the trial. The communists were so frightened that they notified Chanler they would claim their constitutional privilege and refuse to testify. They went back to New Hampshire, unheard.

What the witnesses were afraid of was that the government, with its congressional committees and grand juries, would entangle them in the same way it had snared Remington.

On February 7, 1951, Remington was found guilty and sentenced to five years in jail and a $2,000 fine. This decision was reversed six months later by the court of appeals. It ordered a new trial on the grounds that the judge's charge to the jury had been faulty.

The government now tried Remington again, this time on entirely new charges. This was the same as admitting that it could not prove Remington had ever been a communist and, therefore, that the entire first indictment and trial had been a mistake.

In the new trial, the government claimed that Remington had perjured himself during the first trial by denying that: (1) he had ever knowingly attended Communist party meetings; (2) he had ever given information to Miss Bentley to which she was not "entitled"; (3) he had ever paid Communist party dues; (4) he had ever asked anyone to join the Communist party; and (5) he had any knowledge of the existence of the Young Communist League at Dartmouth College, where he had been a student from 1934 to 1939.

On April 15, 1953, Remington was convicted on two of the five counts of perjury: on count two, that he had given information to Miss Bentley to which she was not entitled; and on count five, that he had knowledge of the Young Communist League at Dartmouth College. He was given a three-year prison sentence.

The basis of his conviction on count two was the testimony of his former wife, forced from her by Donegan and Brunini. The testimony was suspect since it did not agree with Miss Bentley's earlier statements that no one had been present when the information was passed. The fifth count was based on a trick question that Donegan had asked Remington during the first trial. "Knowledge of" the Young Communist League could include hearsay knowledge; in other words, Remington may have heard talk about the league or read about it. When he denied "knowledge of" it, he meant that he had not been a member. It could easily be proved that he knew of it. What made this even more bizarre was that the judge at the first trial had ruled that even if Remington had *belonged* to the Young Communist League, that could not be used to prove he had been a communist.

Remington entered the federal penitentiary at Lewisburg to serve his sentence, and his lawyers appealed his case all the way to the Supreme Court, with no success. On the morning of November 22, 1954, three convicts apparently bent on robbery entered Remington's cell and beat him on the head with a brick wrapped in cloth. He died on the operating table of the prison hospital.

Two months later, the attorney general of New Hampshire gave his state legislature a report based on an eighteen-month investigation of communist activities at Dartmouth. He quoted testimony that Remington, while at Dartmouth, had never been a communist. One witness had even said that communists at Dartmouth at that time had not wanted to have anything to do with Remington "because he was considered too erratic as to timing and sense of responsibility."

Remington was only one of dozens of capable people driven from government service in the 1950s as the loyalty program became subject to political pressure. Foremost in fanning the flames of suspicion was Senator Joseph McCarthy of Wisconsin. He made a career out of trumpeting wild charges of communists in the State Department and other high places.

His Senate Internal Security Subcommittee, like the House Un-American Activities Committee, received much help from the FBI, and McCarthy was given a lot of personal advice and assistance by Director Hoover who, according to writer Ralph de Toledano, "spent many hours . . . lecturing him on Communist strategy and tactics . . . and pointing him in the direction of suspected individuals."

All through this "red-hunting" era, Director Hoover made public statements and published magazine articles and books about the menace of America's communists. FBI files are supposed to be kept confidential, both to protect the identity of the informers and the reputations of those informed on, who are subjects of possibly wild and unsubstantiated stories. The rules guarding these files were broken repeatedly, in spirit, if not technically. Reports extracted from the files by FBI men were given to congressional committees and to unofficial anti-communist groups that, like lesser McCarthys, hounded actors, broadcasters, newsmen, screen writers, and entertainers. The statements of some of the professional "red-hunters" exceeded the bounds of reason. J. B. Matthews, a consultant to congressional committees, accused movie star Shirley Temple of patronizing a French communist newspaper. Walter Steele, another consultant, warned that the Boy Scouts were in danger of a communist takeover. No reputation was safe from rumors and fantasies.

File data found their way to Congress and others, in the form of copies of letters sent by the bureau to various government offices. Many of these letters were sent to cabinet members by Hoover, who felt called upon to warn them of communists, or suspected communists, whether asked to do so or not. The bureau's director also quoted from these secret files in his book *Masters of Deceit*.

Violations of constitutional rights were just as flagrant as during the Palmer raids, only this time the dirty work was done with the help of congressional committees.

Was the loyalty program worth all the anguish it caused, the hysteria and witch-hunting it encouraged by example? Of the 2.3 million employees checked, 76 were discharged and 2,149 others quietly resigned. Even if all really were loyalty risks—which they were not—the proportion of bad apples was one out of a thousand.

Did the methods used secure our Constitution, or would we have been better off had the FBI just kept those suspected of disloyalty under surveillance and made arrests when overt acts were committed?

Liberty and order will never be *perfectly* safe, until a trespass on the constitutional provisions for either shall be felt with the same keenness that resents an invasion of the dearest rights, until every citizen shall . . . espy, and . . . avenge the unhallowed deed.

— JAMES MADISON in the *National Gazette*, January 19, 1792

The Case of the Reluctant Witnesses

BACKGROUND

Some Americans have had their constitutional rights violated by the FBI. Others have called on the bureau to enforce their rights. This has been particularly true of blacks, who have been largely disappointed in their efforts to have the bureau play an active role in seeing that they were given their constitutional rights (under the Fourteenth and Fifteenth amendments) and treated under the law the same as other Americans.

Following the Civil War, strong laws were passed giving the federal government authority to punish those who deprived black citizens of their newly won rights. But until the late 1950s, the political climate of the nation was such that these laws were ignored; most blacks were left in a limbo somewhere between slavery and freedom. One law, for example, made it a crime for people to conspire to deprive others of due process of the law. But when lynch mobs took the law into their own hands, to burn or hang blacks alleged to have committed crimes, the courts ruled that as private individuals, mobs could not be touched. The federal law, they said, could be used only in cases of violations of due process by government officials.

Even when the law clearly gave the Justice Department authority to investigate a violation—which meant authority for its investigative arm, the FBI—there was little the bureau could do against the entrenched power of racists, both in Washington and in many states, at every level of government.

In 1947, for example, the FBI investigated the lynching of Willie Earle in South Carolina. A mob had broken into the Pickens County jail where Earle was being held as a suspect in the fatal stabbing of a cab driver. The investigation was authorized in the belief that a law-enforcement official—a jailer—had helped the mob by willingly turning over the victim. The FBI and local police arrested twenty-eight persons, twenty-six of whom confessed to having taken part in the lynching. Even with the cooperation of the South Carolina government, all twenty-eight were freed by the jury.

The difficulty in prosecuting such cases, and the hostility that such investigations often aroused, made this an area in which the FBI showed little interest. Then, as the black civil rights movement gained strength in the early 1960s and militants began demonstrating and demanding their rights, the bureau put them in the category of troublemakers. In October 1961, it started a new program to "expose, disrupt, misdirect, discredit or otherwise neutralize the activities" of what were called "black nationalists."

Among the targets of this program was Dr. Martin Luther King, Jr., who was subjected to intensive wiretapping and bugging aimed at discrediting him. The FBI secretly and illegally sent Dr. King's wife, Coretta, a tape recording intended

★ 49

to embarrass him and destroy his marriage. A retired Atlanta FBI agent, Arthur Murtagh, has reported that the bureau tried to disrupt plans for a banquet honoring Dr. King when he won the Nobel prize, and sought to keep him from receiving honorary degrees from universities by planting malicious stories about his personal life, including charges that he diverted to his own use funds of the Southern Christian Leadership Conference, which he headed. The bureau sent in false fire-alarm reports to stop meetings at which he spoke, and made anonymous telephone calls to Dr. King's friends. After Dr. King was assassinated in 1968, the bureau tried to forge letters to hurt the careers of those who took over his organization.

The result of all this nefarious activity, according to the head of the African Heritage Studies Association, Dr. James Turner of Cornell University, is that the development of black leadership and unity in this country was blocked.

At the same time that the FBI was secretly trying to destroy the black civil rights movement, it was coming under public pressure to help the movement. Political opinion in the country changed, and the Justice Department started urging the FBI to act, after demonstrators were set upon by angry mobs while local police did nothing.

That the bureau could be effective in such cases was quickly demonstrated. In 1964, following the murder of three young civil rights workers from the North—James Chaney, Andrew Goodman, and Michael Schwerner—the bureau opened a new field office in Jackson, Mississippi. Within a short time, the FBI not only found their murderers, but it also solved a year-old civil rights beating, helped catch ten men who had bombed sixteen Negro churches and homes, and secured the arrests of those who had killed two blacks whose dismembered bodies had been found in a river.

These successes all came with the help of informers who infiltrated the White Knights, as the local Ku Klux Klan was called. Further acts of terror were prevented by the simple measure of having all 480 members of the Klan interviewed by FBI agents, "just to let them know we know who they are," as Director Hoover said.

The FBI, clearly, was capable of disrupting almost any movement, whether aimed at furthering civil rights or hindering them. The fact that the black civil rights movement was peaceful, and the Klan was violent, seemed to make no difference to the bureau—it treated them alike. Its apparent lack of ability to tell movements that violated the rights of others from those that did not shows that to let the bureau decide for itself which groups to infiltrate is an error.

The bureau, of course, is supposed to be under the control of the Justice Department. The nature of this control, and its problem in the area of civil rights, can be judged from the following tale.

A chilly winter night in central South Carolina. A bonfire blazes in the middle of a street. Beyond the fire, on the far side of the street, rises a four-foot embankment, the edge of a college campus.

There is shouting in the dark, from the direction of the campus, and the dim figures of hundreds of angry students can be seen milling around. Once in a while a few dash forward and throw some big pieces of wood on the fire, shutters or banisters torn from a nearby empty house.

The street with the bonfire is full of armed men in steel helmets: National Guardsmen and police form the state highway patrol. Some of them walk along the railroad tracks that run beside the street on the other side from the embankment. Others huddle along a warehouse beyond the tracks or crouch next to the embankment, nervously peering at the students. There is a warlike atmosphere, an invisible mist, the greasy smell of loaded weapons and the shifting glances of men waiting for something bad to happen.

It is Thursday, February 8, 1968. The time, 9:30 P.M. The name of the college is South Carolina State College, at Orangeburg, South Carolina. It, and neighboring Claflin College, are for black students.

Orangeburg is a small city in the middle of the state of South Carolina. Situated on a fork of the Edisto River and surrounded by cotton farms, it is generally a peaceful place with humming textile plants and lumber mills and the busy ringing of cash registers in supermarkets and the clatter of ten pins in the bowling alley.

The trouble had started Tuesday night in downtown Orangeburg when a bunch of South Carolina State students entered a bowling alley, All Star Lanes. The restaurants, movie houses, and bus station in Orangeburg had long been integrated, and bowling alleys in other South Carolina cities allowed blacks to bowl. But the All Star Lanes, despite efforts of city officials, remained closed to blacks.

The owner of the bowling alley called the police, and fifteen students were arrested. Others went back to the Claflin and South Carolina State campuses and returned with about three hundred more students. They found the Lanes locked and guarded by twenty police officers. An uneasy truce, during which fire trucks equipped with hoses appeared on the scene, was broken when one student kicked in some glass beside the door to the bowling alley. The police moved in swinging clubs, and one student sprayed something into a policeman's eyes that was to permanently damage his sight. The police were alarmed, and the demonstrators were outraged that several girl students were beaten.

The students retreated toward their campuses, throwing bricks, rocks, and sticks along the way, damaging stores, homes, and automobiles.

All through Wednesday and Thursday, feeling on the campuses built up as National Guardsmen and members of the state highway patrol rushed to the city. By Thursday evening, there were 450 National Guardsmen in Orangeburg, in addition to 127 state highway patrolmen. The streets around the colleges were blocked off to protect passing motorists from rocks, and about a hundred armed Guardsmen and state highway patrolmen were stationed in front of the campus on the street that led to downtown Orangeburg.

The students had wanted to stage a protest march through the city, but the mayor had denied them permission. The heads of the two colleges ordered them to stay on their campuses, where they were faced with soldiers and patrolmen standing guard.

Now it was ten o'clock Thursday evening, and the bonfire was blazing in the middle of Watson Street, right in front of the embankment.

The students kept moving back and forth across the five hundred feet of grounds that separated one of the dormitories, Lowman Hall, from Watson Street where the bonfire blazed. They yelled insults at the police.

Officers of the highway patrol, trained in riot control, watched the students from the embankment, the bonfire flickering eerily behind them. Others had crept up the embankment to some bushes that stood between the empty house and the campus. The house belonged to an elderly lady who lived in a nursing home, and the police were there to prevent students from damaging it further.

All of a sudden something happened to Officer David Shealy. He was felled at the embankment, and there was blood all over his mouth.

The next moment, the patrolmen along the embankment started to fire shotguns, carbines, and pistols into the moving crowd of students. The shotguns were loaded with buckshot, large lead pellets the size of a .22 caliber bullet. It was powerful stuff, used for killing deer and other big game.

In a few minutes, thirty students were hit. Of these, three received fatal wounds and died soon afterward.

Why had the police opened fire? They claimed that they

had first been fired on by the students. They said that Officer Shealy appeared to have been shot in the head. They had, they said, fired in self-defense.

This was the way the story appeared in newspapers all over the country. The students had been killed "during a heavy exchange of gunfire" in which a patrolman had been "struck in the head by a bullet."

It soon came out that Officer Shealy had not been hit by a bullet, but by a heavy banister that someone had thrown down at him from the embankment. But the governor of South Carolina, Robert McNair, still blamed the deaths on the students. The actions leading to the three deaths and numerous injuries, he stated, came only after an extended period of sniper fire from the campus and "not until an officer had been felled during his efforts to protect life and property."

Two victims lie on the ground while members of the South Carolina State Highway Patrol look on. (*United Press International*)

A college dean who had witnessed the confrontation said he had heard no shooting by students.

On Friday evening, U.S. Attorney General Ramsey Clark telephoned Governor McNair to tell him that he was asking the FBI to make an investigation. This was welcomed by the governor. He believed what he had said, which was based on the reports of state police at the scene, and he was certain the investigation would show that his men had done the right thing.

Attorney General Clark's interest in the case stemmed from its civil rights aspects—from the fact that all the victims were black and that all the policemen were white.

The focus of the investigation was on what had happened just before the police had opened fire. If they had been fired upon, they had opened fire legally in self-defense. If they had not been fired upon, then they had used far more force than was necessary and had violated the civil rights of the students. Whether a lawful police action or murder had taken place that Thursday night rested on the testimony of people who had been on Watson Street with the police when they opened fire.

Two months after the shooting, the FBI submitted a report based on interviews with the sixty-six highway patrolmen who had been at the scene, including nine who admitted that they had fired their weapons. Eight of these patrolmen said that shots had come from the students just before they opened fire.

The FBI report, based on the testimony of the local police, supported the official South Carolina version of what had happened, but the Justice Department wasn't satisfied. It did not seem that much effort had been made to find independent witnesses or to gather evidence. Shotguns had been fired, but the FBI search of the area produced no shells.

In May, a young Justice Department attorney, Charles Quaintance, took a trip to Orangeburg to see what he could find out. The Civil Rights Division of the Justice Department suspected that the local FBI men had not been thorough because of their close working relationship with the South Carolina police. Agent-in-charge Charles DeFord worked very closely with the Special Law Enforcement Division (SLED) and was friendly with its chief, F. P. Strom, who had been the highest South Carolina official at the scene of the shooting. And Agent Nelson Phillips had instructed the state highway patrolmen who fired the shots in riot-control tactics. A third FBI man, Bill Danielson, had been in Orangeburg keeping surveillance on Cleveland Sellers, Jr., a SNCC (Students Nonviolent Co-ordinating Committee) organizer who was working on the South Carolina State campus.

When Justice Department lawyers had interviewed the three agents in February, the agents told them they had no firsthand knowledge of what had happened.

But Charles Quaintance learned that *the three FBI agents had been at the scene of the shooting.* They therefore had firsthand knowledge of what had happened; and their testimony, either supporting or contradicting that of the patrolmen, should have been in the report.

Agent-in-charge DeFord, who had been standing with Chief Strom of SLED, had neither seen nor heard any shots fired by the students.

Agent Phillips had been with the highway patrolmen when they shot the students. He said that he had heard some small-arms fire from the campus just before the patrolmen fired their weapons.

Agent Danielson had gone behind a boxcar across the street from the highway patrolmen because, he said, he believed shots were being fired by the students.

No evidence was ever found that any shots had been fired at the police just before they fired on the students. Some shots had been fired about an *hour* before, but when the .22 caliber slugs were dug out of the side of the warehouse behind where some patrolmen had been standing and were examined at the FBI laboratory in Washington, it was shown that they had not come from the direction of the State College campus.

Clearly, the three FBI agents at the scene had not been honest with the Justice Department. They did not put in the report that they themselves had been observers, or even mention that they had been on the scene.

Attorney Quaintance also found some of the shotgun shells. These were very important pieces of evidence, since they could be used to identify which weapons had been fired. The agents could easily have found them in February, had they wanted to, since a free-lance photographer had had no trouble finding some.

The FBI had a reputation for carefully collecting evidence. When an agent testified in a courtroom, he was usually well supplied with facts, precise, and to the point. Director Hoover boasted of the number of convictions that resulted in cases the bureau brought to trial, and this record was based on the thoroughness of the special agents. When they testified to something, they had the evidence to back up their words. But in this case they acted more like witnesses for the defense than for the prosecution. For example, the commander of the state highway patrolmen who fired the shots, Lieutenant Jesse Spell, and the patrolmen as well, all made a point of testifying that the lieutenant had ordered them to fire, to show that they had acted under orders.

When Attorney Quaintance questioned FBI Agent Phillips about this in a courtroom, he found it difficult to get any clear information.

Q. Mr. Phillips, have you talked to any of the defendants about the case?

A. I don't know specifically, sir, I talked to them every day, but about the case, no, sir. . . .

Q. Do you know the defendants?

A. I know most of them, yes, sir.

Q. Have you ever—just about this incident though specifically, do you recall having talked to any of them about it?

A. Yes, sir, I talked to almost all of them immediately there-

THE **FBI** AND THE **CIA**

after for one reason or another, sir. Because I had liaison with their departments. I had to set up interviews and things of this nature.

Q. Do you recall the first time that we spoke concerning the incident, you and I?

A. Yes, sir, May 1968, sir.

Q. And at that time did I ask you whether you had talked to any of the patrolmen about the incident?

A. Yes, sir, I do.

Q. Did you at that time, the first time we talked . . . did you tell me that you would not tell me what they had said?

A. No, sir, I did not. . . .

Q. Do you recall for example telling me that, that Lieutenant Spell told you he had not himself given an order, but that he was going to tell the agents that he had because he was afraid that somebody had misinterpreted what another person had said?

A. I remember you and I discussing it, yes, sir.

Q. Did Lieutenant Spell say something like that?

A. We discussed some stuff, yes, sir. We discussed the fact of authority, who was in charge of that squad. . . . As to the exact wording, I don't recall, Mr. Quaintance.

Why did the FBI agents not help the Justice Department more? The explanation is complicated. For one thing, Agents DeFord and Phillips worked closely with the South Carolina police on all sorts of other cases.

In bank robberies, kidnappings, and other criminal activities, the police and the FBI are on the same side. Many local police take courses at the FBI's National Police Academy and use many FBI services in the course of their work. They send fingerprints to Washington to be checked against FBI files and rely on the bureau for other information that will help them catch criminals.

Without such close cooperation, both state and federal

police would be hampered in their anticrime work. In civil rights cases, where local police may be part of the problem, this cooperation is threatened. An FBI agent who does his job and helps his superiors prosecute those who violate civil rights may be helping prosecute local police. He is put on the spot. If the agent does his job, he will lose the friendship of local police with whom he has built a valuable working partnership. If he sides with the police, he risks discipline by the bureau. Agents DeFord and Phillips chose to stick by the South Carolina State Highway Patrol and the State Law Enforcement Division.

Agent Danielson was in a different position. As part of the massive FBI effort to destroy the black civil rights movement, he had been assigned to watch SNCC organizer Cleveland Sellers. When he followed Sellers to downtown Orangeburg on Tuesday night, he reported that Sellers had played a big part in stirring up trouble.

Danielson continued seeing Sellers as a ringleader in all the events that followed. Yet, as reporters Jack Nelson and Jack Bass showed in their excellent book *The Orangeburg Massacre,* the bowling-alley agitation was inspired by two students: a league bowler, John Stroman, who had become sick and tired of driving forty miles to Columbia every time he wanted to bowl; and James P. Davis, an air force veteran. Sellers, they found, had organized a group of black activists on the campus, but being an outsider, he had very little influence.

Preventing the kind of violence that erupted in Orangeburg is a worthwhile objective. But the prevention of such outbreaks requires a deeper understanding of people and their motives than was shown by the FBI. Nor should prevention have been entrusted to a bureau that, by engaging in an illegal program of disruption, had become part of the problem it was being asked to solve.

Since the general civilization of mankind, I believe there are more instances of the abridgement of the freedom of the people, by gradual and silent encroachments of those in power, than by violent and sudden usurpations.
—JAMES MADISON in the Virginia Convention, June 6, 1788

Big Brother Has Your Record

BACKGROUND

Big Brother is the "benevolent" leader whose picture appears everywhere in the England of George Orwell's frightening vision of the future, 1984. Big Brother or his agents literally watch everyone through television cameras that are almost everywhere—even in people's homes, built into their television sets. No one can be sure, no matter where he is, that Big Brother is not watching.

The surveillance is done for everyone's benefit. Criminals and troublemakers are restrained because of fear of being caught in the act. But no one is free.

Surveillance, whether by tapping telephones, planting microphones (bugs), shadowing, or secretly opening mail, is often done for good reasons. But because it requires secrecy, it can be easily done for any reason. Almost every FBI field office has a "SUTECH" (Technical Surveillance) room in which a tape recorder will start whirring as soon as someone in another part of the city picks up a telephone. That someone may be a suspected gambler, a drug dealer, the father of a kidnapped child, a local diplomatic mission, the office of a political group suspected of having foreign connections, or a member of a criminal syndicate.

The number the caller dials is printed out on a long sheet of paper, and then the entire conversation is recorded. Everything on the tapes is typed out by clerks, and the logs are sent to the bureau's huge "ELSUR" (Electronic Surveillance) files in Washington, where they may remain for a hundred years.

Surveillance and record keeping, like many other agency functions described in this book, have a good side—they can help catch wrongdoers and even prevent crimes—and a bad side—they can violate precious constitutional rights.

Whether or not they are used to good purpose depends on how they are controlled. The FBI until recently could wiretap anyone's phone at the request of the Attorney General. Some former FBI agents have suggested that the Attorney General's permission was not always obtained. A law passed in 1968 made it necessary for the bureau to get a federal court order to wiretap a telephone in a criminal case. Where national security is at issue, it may still go ahead without an order if a foreign government is involved. In the case of "bugs," no court's permission is needed.

With regard to the keeping of records, Congress in 1930 passed a law giving the Attorney General the right to collect information on criminals and to share it with other branches of the federal government and with states and cities. The whole idea behind this was to aid in the capture of criminals. Fingerprints found at the scene of a bank robbery in Omaha, for example, might not match any prints on file in the state of Nebraska but could belong to a felon once arrested in California.

When the members of Congress wrote the law, they

clearly intended to limit use of the records to law enforcement. But as so often happens, the actions of bureaucrats have distorted the original intention.

In Los Angeles at 3:45 A.M., Tuesday, August 10, 1965, a prowler was seen looking in the rear window of a sanatorium. He appeared young and was wearing dark clothes.

Police officers arriving at the scene at 4:00 A.M. looked through the parking lot in back of the sanatorium, then checked out the surrounding area. They spotted a man lying on a park bench. He was wearing dark clothes and needed a shave.

They asked the man on the bench his name.

"Dale Menard."

On the ground near the bench was a wallet. They looked in the wallet and saw that it belonged to someone else. There was a ten-dollar bill inside. Deducing that Menard was the prowler and that he has just stolen the wallet and thrown it on the ground as they approached, the police arrested him for burglary and took him to the station house.

Police are not allowed to arrest just anybody. They must have a good reason. On the basis of what they had heard and seen, they believed it likely that Menard had committed a crime. They had what is technically called "probable cause" for arresting him as a burglary suspect.

Dale Menard was nineteen years old. He had never been arrested before.

No one had reported a burglary in the area to the police. The charge was just based on the complaint of prowling. Menard denied knowing anything about the wallet. The police could find no evidence that he had done anything wrong. Two days later he was released. No charges were placed against him.

Dale Menard was once again a free man. Or was he?

At the time of his arrest, Menard was fingerprinted. His

fingerprints, along with a notice of his arrest, were sent to the FBI's Identification Bureau in Washington in accordance with a regular procedure in which the fingerprints of all persons arrested anywhere in the United States are sent to the bureau.

In return for receiving these fingerprints, which are used in making a central file of criminals, the bureau sends back any information already in its files on the criminal records of the person who has been fingerprinted. The bureau had nothing on Menard, so nothing came back to Los Angeles. But after he was released, Menard's fingerprints and the notice stating that he had been arrested remained in the files of the FBI's National Crime Information Center.

> Date of arrested or received: 8/10/65
> Charge or offense: 459 [Probable Cause] Burglary
> Disposition or sentence: 8/12/65. Released. Unable to connect with any felony or misdemeanor at this time.
> Occupation: student
> Residence of person fingerprinted: Saticoy and Canoga, Canoga Park

Menard thought that this record ought to be removed from the FBI's criminal files. He had done nothing wrong, yet he was listed in the files of the National Crime Information Center (NCIC). He wasn't sure who might see this record. It was possible, for example, that he might be arrested again, just by being in the wrong place or looking suspicious. But this time, when he was fingerprinted, the police would get back from Washington a record that would make him look like a criminal. Even worse, others besides police departments might see his record, and this might get him in all sorts of trouble.

Most people think that anyone whose record is in the National Crime Information Center is a criminal. A story in the July 17, 1966, *New York Times,* for example, referred to those whose fingerprints are sent to the FBI after arrest as "criminals." Most employment agencies do not accept as job applicants anyone with an *arrest* record.

Dale Menard's family wrote to the Los Angeles Police Department asking that his arrest record be removed from its files and from those of the FBI in Washington. After six months of letters, they were finally told that the record could be removed only "upon order of a court of competent jurisdiction."

Dale Menard enlisted in the Marine Corps, served his time, and became an officer. Discharged from service, and having moved to Silver Spring, Maryland, he got in touch with the Department of Justice about having his record expunged. The department said that it had "no authority" to do this, so he decided to apply to "a court of competent jurisdiction."

He chose the federal court covering the District of Columbia and sued Attorney General John Mitchell and FBI Director J. Edgar Hoover to remove his arrest records from the identification files of the FBI.

He argued that since he had not been convicted of any crime, the keeping and using "of his arrest record for any purpose whatsoever violates several Constitutional guarantees—the presumption of innocence, due process, the right to privacy, and the freedom from unreasonable search under the Fourth Amendment."

It took a long time for the courts to reach a decision. The first judge who heard the case, Federal District Judge Aubrey Robinson, Jr., ruled against Menard. But his ruling was reversed by the three-judge court of appeals. It sent the case back to the lower court because it recognized that Menard had raised a question that had never before come up in court. There simply was not enough known about what the FBI did with its criminal records to be able to decide if Menard's complaint made sense.

Congress had passed laws that said how the records were supposed to be used. If the records were used only in accordance with the law, then there was nothing that the court could do for Menard. But, as Judge Bazelon of the court of appeals noted, no one knew if, in fact, the FBI did use the records only in accordance with the law. On the one hand, there wasn't any exact information on who was allowed to see what was in the criminal files. On the other hand, there were plenty of ways Menard could be hurt if the files got into the wrong hands. His arrest record could keep him from getting into school or from getting a job or a professional license. If he had some further difficulty with the law, it could make it harder for him to be left free on bail before trial.

Menard could be injured, Judge Bazelon thought, in two different ways. He could be hurt if his record were shown to people who had no right to see it. And he could be hurt if his record, which concerned a mere arrest, were treated in the same manner as one showing a conviction. "There is a limit beyond which the government may not tread," Bazelon said, "in . . . lump[ing] the innocent with the guilty."

The court could not know whether or not Menard was right in worrying about his record without knowing the facts about what the FBI did with its records. Judge Bazelon and his two colleagues therefore asked the lower court to get the facts. To find out: (1) who, according to law, was authorized to see records like Menard's; (2) who, in actual practice, did see them and how the FBI prevented unauthorized use of its files; (3) why the Justice Department claimed it had no authority to remove records from its files when they concerned persons not guilty of any crime.

The lower court that the case went back to was presided over by Judge Gerhard Gesell instead of by Judge Robinson, who had heard the case the first time. Armed with the appeals court's request, Judge Gesell ordered the men in charge of the FBI's criminal files to appear in court to answer questions. It was in his court that, for the first time, the use the FBI made of its criminal files was revealed.

The answers given by the FBI showed that the situation was at least as bad as anyone had dreaded. It wasn't that the

FBI was trying to give out unauthorized information from these criminal files, or to ruin anyone's reputation. It was just that the situation had gotten entirely out of control.

As the FBI explained it, its files contained almost 200 million sets of fingerprints for about 100 million people. These arrived at the rate of 29,000 sets a day. Of these, 13,000, a bit less than half, were in connection with arrests and were from law-enforcement agencies (police departments). The latter went into the criminal files of the NCIC, which contained records of 60 million arrests involving about 19 million people.

With regard to the information in these "criminal" files, it was up to those who sent in the fingerprints to keep them up to date. A fingerprint set came in with a notice of arrest. From then on, the local police force that sent the prints was supposed to tell the FBI whether the person was found guilty of a crime or released. Menard's record noted that he had been "Released. Unable to connect with any felony or misdemeanor at this time." This was the case because he had only been held for two days. Another person with charges brought against him might be out on bail for months before trial. His record would show the arrest, but might not show how the case was settled. The person could have been found innocent, but the record might show only that he was arrested.

The availability of these files, containing often incomplete information, was also out of control.

As the court had stated, the use of FBI files had been defined by the Congress. The Identification Division was set up in 1924. Laws passed by Congress in 1930 and after clearly stated that the division was to be limited to the collection and keeping of "criminal identification and other crime records." Congressmen, fearing misuse of the files, limited their use to law-enforcement purposes. However, of the 8,000 agencies that now send fingerprints to the FBI, half have nothing to do with law enforcement as the term was understood by Congress when it set up the system in 1930.

What happened was that, once the system was in operation, different attorneys general had made rulings that said the FBI could collect and exchange data with insurance companies, railroad police, national banks and other banks, and from "other governmental agencies."

These other "governmental agencies" came to include cities that required fingerprints from anyone applying for a taxi license or who wished to operate a bar. Some counties began requesting fingerprints from everyone who applied for a municipal job. As the number of those sending in fingerprints increased, so did the number of those authorized to get information from the FBI files, for the FBI did not distinguish between police departments or any of the others sending in fingerprints, whether banks, counties, or hack-license bureaus. Its criminal files were available to anyone who was authorized to send it fingerprints, for whatever reason.

Nor did the bureau have any control over the use of this information once it sent it out. It tried to prevent misuse by instructing recipients that the information was for "official business only"; but it had no way of checking on whether this instruction was followed.

For example, the town of Manaplan, Florida, passed a law requiring that all domestics be fingerprinted. As soon as it did this, the town made itself eligible to receive records from the FBI's criminal files on anyone who worked in the town as a maid, cook, or butler, or on anyone who applied for such a job. Even if the town office, without revealing the contents of the records, just passed on the fact that a certain domestic or applicant had a record, employers would be finding out more than they had a right to know.

It also became clear that the FBI did not make any distinction between those who were merely arrested and those who were convicted. The place in which the records were kept was the National *Crime* Information Center, and the FBI called those whose records were there a "criminal army."

About half the soldiers in this "criminal army" had been merely arrested. Many, like Menard, had never been prosecuted; others had been found innocent after trial.

Arrests could be for reasons that had nothing to do with crime. Arrests were often used as a means of annoying civil rights workers or other protesters of various sorts; they had become increasingly common in the era of antiwar and civil rights protest. Sometimes, arrests were made of those just watching a protest. Early in 1970, for example, forty people were arrested during a protest march on the Watergate apartments in Washington. Many of the arrested had done nothing. They had, in fact, been trying to move on, as directed by the police, when they were picked up. Yet every one of these people was fingerprinted at the police station and placed on file in the NCIC.

What such an arrest record could mean to a person was shown when the state of New York passed a law requiring that all who worked for Wall Street firms be fingerprinted. Of the several hundred employees who lost their jobs because they were found to have "criminal records," *half* had never been convicted of anything.

The New York law did not say that a person whose record showed that he had been merely arrested had to be dismissed. The bosses who made the decisions simply did not distinguish between the convicted and those who had not been found guilty.

This use of *arrest* records as if they were *criminal* records of convictions, then, could lead to a lot of injustice even if the use of the records was carefully controlled, which it was not.

The reader will recall that Judge Bazelon's court sought the answers to several questions. Not only did it want to know how the FBI controlled its criminal records, it also wanted to know why the Justice Department claimed it had no authority to remove records from its files where they concerned persons who had merely been arrested.

With regard to this second question, Judge Gesell, following the Justice Department's argument, agreed that criminal records could be wiped out only by court order and that the only court that could properly decide the meaning of an arrest was a court that functioned in the place where the arrest was made. Since Menard had been arrested under California law, only a California court could order that the record be expunged, first from the California files and then from those of the FBI.

With regard to the other questions raised by the court of appeals, Judge Gesell found that much of the use to which the records were put went far beyond the intention of the laws authorizing the FBI to collect criminal information. As he wrote, "Congress never intended to or in fact did authorize dissemination of arrest records to any state or local agency for purposes of employment of licensing. . . . Neither the statute nor the debates so much as mention employment, and it is beyond reason to assume that Congress intended that this confidential . . . data should be handed to anyone who under authorization of local ordinance . . . was authorized to take a fingerprint from an applicant for a position in public or private employment. . . . With the increasing availability of fingerprints, technological developments, and the enormous increase in population, the system is out of . . . control. The Bureau needs legislative guidance. . . . It is not the function of the courts to make these judgments, but the courts must call a halt until the legislature acts. Thus the Court finds that the *Bureau is without authority to disseminate arrest records outside the Federal Government for employment, licensing or related purposes* [italics added] whether or not the record reflects a later conviction."

The whole subject, the court thought, raised fundamental questions regarding our liberties. Privacy had been considered a basic right since the beginning of the nation. "A heavy burden is placed on all branches of Government," it said, "to keep a proper balance between collecting information and the necessity to safeguard privacy. The systematic collection of records and dissemination of information about individual citizens is a form of surveillance and control which may easily inhibit freedom to speak, to work, and to move about in this land. If information available to Government is misused to publicize past incidents in the lives of its citizens the pressures for conformity will be irresistible. . . . In short the overwhelming power of the Federal Government to expose must be held in proper check."

The decision, particularly Judge Gesell's words that "the Bureau is without authority to disseminate arrest records outside the Federal Government for employment, licensing or related purposes whether or not the record reflects a later conviction" virtually halted dissemination of records by the NCIC.

However, the bureau was soon able to resume its former practice of sending arrest and other records to all sorts of non-law-enforcement agencies. It prevailed on Congress to tack a rider onto a Justice Department appropriations bill. Meanwhile, some congressmen, alerted by what had come out in Judge Gesell's courtroom, have been trying to draw up new legislation that would permit legitimate use of criminal records while preventing abuses.

These abuses may, in fact, be causing the criminal files to have results opposite to those intended. They may be increasing crime, rather than diminishing it. Our system of criminal justice is based on the idea that people can be reformed. A record of a past misdeed, seen by a credit agency or an employer, could make it impossible for a person to buy a home or get a job. The record, by preventing the person from having an equal chance, could make it hard for him not to return to a life of crime.

The misuse of the FBI's criminal files came about because, until the Menard case, no one outside the bureau knew exactly what was being done with the criminal records. As long

★ 70

as government agencies can conceal their practices, illegal encroachments on such constitutional rights as privacy will occur. "Big Brother" will come, watching and remembering our every move, unless we practice eternal vigilance. Things are happening, in secret, all the time.

For the past several years, for example, the FBI has been trying to create a huge communications system that would not only connect its central data bank in the NCIC with those of all the country's local police departments, but would also enable it to control the flow of information between them.

The prospect of such a centralization of criminal information has horrified both conservative, law-enforcement-prone senators like Roman L. Hruska of Nebraska and those, like John V. Tunney of California, more concerned with individual rights. In May 1974, Attorney General William Saxbe agreed to hold up implementation of this plan until Senator Sam Ervin's civil rights subcommittee, of which Hruska and Tunney are members, had a chance to write new laws controlling the NCIC.

Despite this agreement, the Justice Department secretly gave the go-ahead to the FBI, a decision that was balked in October 1974 when it was exposed by White House aide John M. Eger. The battle continues. As of July 1975, no new legislation had been passed, and the FBI was still trying to get the Justice Department to go ahead. Only the vigilance of senators and their committee staffs prevented the tentacles of the FBI from reaching into the communications brains of every law-enforcement agency in the country.

Men who injure and oppress the people under their administration provoke them to cry out and complain; and then make that very complaint the foundation for new oppressions and persecutions.

—ANDREW HAMILTON in defense of John Peter Zenger, 1735

Director Hoover's Revenge

BACKGROUND

Starting in 1908 with 20 full-time special agents, the FBI had, by 1970, more than 7,500 agents operating out of 59 major offices and 500 smaller offices. It also had 10,000 other employees and an annual budget of more than $300 million.

Internal security, dropped by the bureau for a dozen years only to be resumed at the urging of President Franklin Roosevelt in 1936, had by 1970 grown into an activity that took about $50 million of the bureau's budget and demanded the services of some 2,000 agents.

It was a giant operation. Millions of people were watched, photographed at demonstrations, informed on at meetings. Security programs, extended to defense industries, covered so many millions of people—at least 20 percent of the work force —that there probably were few Americans whose investigation could not be justified on one ground or another. Investigations of suspected employees led to probes of friends and acquaintances. Probes of subversive organizations led to planting informers in whatever groups members of the subversive groups belonged to. The net was wide, embracing opponents of government policies along with opponents of the government itself. During the Vietnam war, antiwar activists were watched along with members of groups plotting violence; Black Power advocates who believed in the Constitution were watched along with those who preached ghetto riots for personal gain.

The excuse for all this was national security, *which, by 1970, had become a kind of state religion. Starting with Franklin Roosevelt, each President had called on the FBI to help protect the nation against internal enemies. The nature of the enemies changed as threats to the United States—at least as perceived by Presidents—changed. In the late 1930s, the greatest threat seemed Nazi Germany, and the German-American Bund and other groups that sought to enlist support for Hitler were the targets of surveillance. In 1940, with the Germans dominating Europe and Roosevelt striving to keep Britain from collapsing, the FBI was put on the trail of the America First Committee. This group was composed of many sorts of people, from conservative bankers to radical labor agitators, united in a desire to keep the country out of the war. As it opposed his efforts to assist Great Britain, President Roosevelt suspected ties between the America First Committee and the Nazi government.*

The Communist party, depicted as the great threat of the late 1940s and 1950s, gradually lost its position as the number one menace to black power groups like the Black Panthers and student radicals like the Weathermen of the 1960s. Presidents came and went, but the FBI continued, growing in numbers and power.

And FBI internal security measures went beyond mere surveillance. Leaders of civil rights and other activist groups were harassed. The Reverend Donald Jackson was hounded out of Mississippi by anonymous letters accusing him of crimes he had never committed. Similar tactics drove Professor Morris Starsky from Arizona State University, where he was an antiwar leader. The sending of letters with false information is a crime, and the FBI sent the letters anonymously to escape punishment. The bureau committed other crimes. Agents and informers who infiltrated meetings proposed illegal actions to cause dissension. Worse, they helped plan and carry out crimes that trapped others.

Much of this illegal activity was part of a secret operation called Cointelpro. It is not clear that anyone except the FBI knew of it, for Director Hoover ordered that it not be revealed "outside the bureau." If, in fact, the bureau was able to undertake such programs without informing anyone, it had come a long way from the original plan described by Attorney General Bonaparte when he promised Congress that he would always know what his agents were doing.

But could the FBI be blamed for becoming so powerful and independent without also blaming the Presidents it served and the Congress that had the power to demand that it reveal whatever it did?

Whether liberty, on balance, gained or lost by all this FBI activity, there is no question that, by 1970, more Americans were being watched by their government than at any time in their history.

The quality of this scrutiny can be judged from the following tale.

Daniel and Philip Berrigan were two Catholic priests. Daniel was small, dark, and intense. Philip, two years younger, was big, burly, and fair. Following different paths, both had come to oppose the Vietnam war. Their opposition brought them into conflict with the U.S. government when they started destroying draft files. They were sentenced to prison for burning 378 files from the draft-board office in Catonsville, Mary-

Fathers Philip and Daniel Berrigan (*left, right*) watch as records they have taken from the draft-board office in Catonsville, Maryland, are incinerated by homemade napalm. May 17, 1968. (*United Press International*)

land, with homemade napalm. On April 9, 1970, they were supposed to turn themselves in, to begin serving their time. Instead, they became fugitives from justice.

The Berrigans were not ordinary fugitives. They had decided to try to stay out of prison not so much to save their own skins, as to enlist others in their cause.

The Berrigans believed that the U.S. government itself, by murdering thousands of Vietnamese people, was lawless and that it was the duty of good men to oppose everything that contributed to the war. "I went to Catonsville and burned some papers," Daniel wrote, "because I had gone to Hanoi. . . . Although I was too old to carry a draft card there were other ways of getting into trouble with a state that seemed determined on multiplying the dead, totally intent upon a war the meaning of which no sane man could tell."

They had willingly been arrested. Reporters had been invited to their draft-files burning in Catonsville, and they had used the trial as a way of spreading their ideas. Now, they decided, their staying out of jail would awaken more people to the need for resistance. Everyone who hid them would be an accomplice to their crime.

They also used their fleeing from the government as a means of calling attention to themselves and their movement. They wanted to show how many friends they had. Four days after they went underground, the Catholic Resistance announced that Daniel Berrigan would appear at a rally at Cornell University on April 19 and that Philip would appear at another rally at St. Gregory's Church in New York City on April 21.

The FBI, charged with finding fugitives, of course took this as a challenge. Ten thousand Cornell students showed up to greet Daniel Berrigan, who appeared in a motorcycle helmet and goggles. The numerous FBI agents, who had decided to nab the priest after he spoke, were very annoyed when, following his speech, the lights were doused and Daniel Berrigan disappeared.

A hundred FBI field agents showed up at St. Gregory's, and Philip was captured.

In that spring of 1970, FBI Director Hoover was seventy-five years old. He had been at his job for forty-six years and had become a law unto himself. Many bureaucrats are retired from government at sixty, others at sixty-five; but Presidents were afraid to ask Hoover to leave. Why this was so can only be guessed at.

One reason could have been that Hoover had long been a favorite of many members of Congress, who revered him as the guardian of the American spirit. Others feared what the FBI knew about them. As a story in the *New York Times* on February 25, 1974, noted, "Congressmen had discreetly but systematically been made aware of 'derogatory' material about themselves that bureau agents had come across."

A "well-placed source" told the *New York Times* that one senator "had been told of an investigation concerning his daughter, a college student who had gotten involved in demonstrations and free love"; and a Republican representative "had been told the bureau possessed evidence indicating that he was a homosexual. 'We had him in our pocket after that,' " the source said of the representative.

Mr. Hoover also had his agents look for damaging information on political opponents of his friends in Congress. He was thus able to help friends as well as threaten opponents.

As a result of this immense power, Director Hoover was able to do as he liked. The FBI's activities against violent or subversive groups were supposed to be carried out under the direction of the President. People assumed that whatever the FBI did was authorized by the President or his Attorney General. In fact, it seems that the FBI did things that no one else knew about, for two previous attorneys general, Nicholas Katzenbach and Ramsey Clark, have both denied any knowledge of the bureau's disruptive Cointelpro operation. "The idea that I would have tolerated any government agent engaging in any disruptive activity," Mr. Clark said, "is false and unthinkable."

It took a great deal of courage, in 1970, for a fugitive from justice to make fun of the FBI. One can imagine how Director Hoover felt when, with the entire bureau out to catch Daniel Berrigan, the fugitive priest appeared on television shows and gave interviews to reporters.

Daniel Berrigan seemed to enjoy his ability to give the bureau the slip. "One of the reasons I'm doing this," he told a reporter for *The New Yorker,* "is to break down the myth of the omnipotence of the people in power. . . . I must say that the FBI are the politest bloodhounds I've ever had on my trail."

On Sunday, August 2, he surfaced at a Methodist Church in Germantown, Pennsylvania, to give a sermon. "Christians," he said, "can aid and abet and harbor people like myself who are in legal jeopardy . . . along with AWOLs . . . we have chosen to be branded peace criminals by war criminals."

The FBI went all-out in its effort to capture the missing priest. Armed with bench warrants that allowed them to enter any place they suspected fugitive Daniel Berrigan to be, they surrounded a hospital in Syracuse where the priest's mother lay ill, searched churches and convents, and even invaded the wedding of the daughter of one of the Berrigans' friends.

Father Daniel kept mocking the FBI. "It's like the U.S. Army, which, with all its material, can't win against the North Vietnamese people," he had told *The New Yorker.* "You could say that my survival is a triumph of love and humanity of the people who shelter me over the FBI, who are merciless but extraordinarily unimaginative men."

This sort of thing must have been very hard for Director Hoover to take. He had been wrapping himself and his bureau in the American flag for so long, and now it seemed a large group of Americans were willing to put loyalty to Daniel Berrigan ahead of loyalty to the bureau and the laws it was trying to enforce. In the eyes of the peace movement, the FBI was not a protector of virtue but a tool of an evil state machine.

The FBI finally caught up with Father Daniel on Block Island, where he was visiting two old friends, William Stringfellow and Anthony Towne, and he went to Danbury Penitentiary in Connecticut. There, on August 25, he was joined by his brother Philip who, up to that time, had been held in Lewisburg Prison in Pennsylvania. (The government brought charges against Stringfellow and Towne, but these were dismissed by a federal judge on technical grounds.)

Both Berrigans, along with those who had joined them in destroying the draft files, were in jail. But the FBI was not through with them.

Three months after Daniel was caught, in November 1970, Director Hoover told a Senate subcommittee that the Berrigans were the leaders of an anarchist group, "The East Coast Conspiracy to Save Lives," that planned to throw the federal government into chaos by blowing up utilities and to kidnap a White House staff member.

In publicly mentioning the plot, Director Hoover was violating Justice Department rules that demanded silence until investigations were completed. A number of other FBI men had asked him not to mention it because it would damage an ongoing investigation.

When Philip Berrigan heard these accusations at Danbury, he decided that "they wanted to bury us in prison for the rest of our lives." Later, he and Daniel issued a press release saying that they had been "tried and condemned by Mr. Hoover's remarks, and we should have an equal opportunity to answer his charges. He ought . . . either to prosecute us or publicly retract the charges."

The Reverend Joseph Wenderoth, a leader of the East Coast Conspiracy to Save Lives, denied that the Berrigans were members and denied that the group had any violent aims.

The Berrigans were also defended by Congressman William R. Anderson of Tennessee, who demanded that the FBI director either face the two priests with formal charges or make a retraction.

Director Hoover's response was to order a massive probe involving hundreds of special agents from Washington, Philadelphia, and New York. A high FBI official told Jack Nelson and Ronald J. Ostrow, authors of *The FBI and the Berrigans,* that Hoover kept urging his men to "pull out all stops." On January 12, 1971, when indictments were finally issued, one of the alleged conspirators was brought to the FBI office in Newark by fifteen agents in five cars. The conspirator was a nun, Sister Elizabeth McAlister.

Even with hundreds of agents working on the case and with all the advantages of using a grand jury in a conspiracy case, the government had a lot of trouble drawing up an indictment.

Grand juries have special powers that put witnesses and possible defendants in a weaker position before them than they are in a court of law. They cannot, as they can in court, bring lawyers with them, nor can they challenge the jury's right to ask questions about any subject. A prosecutor in a courtroom must show that his question is related to the crime at issue. A grand jury can go on a "fishing expedition," searching for evidence without knowing whether or not a crime has been committed. Nor does the grand jury have to follow any strict rules of evidence. Hearsay—something a witness has heard from a third party—is admitted in a court of law only if corroborated by at least two other persons. In a grand jury, an indictment for crime can be based on unsupported hearsay evidence.

Conspiracy charges make the grand jury's task even easier. A conspiracy to break the law is as unlawful as actually breaking the law. It means that more than one person has *planned* to break the law.

In a conspiracy case, the conspirators may actually have gone ahead and broken the law, in which case they could be charged with actual violations as well. Or they may not yet have reached the stage of actually doing anything. Strangely, it is easier to bring a charge against a conspirator who has not yet actually taken action than it is to bring one against a person who has taken action who is *not* a conspirator. The reason for this is that the rules for evidence in conspiracy cases are not nearly as strict as in cases involving actual lawbreaking.

First of all, the grand jury in Harrisburg, Pennsylvania, charged six people with conspiracy to break two federal laws. The first offense, a conspiracy "to blow up the heating system of federal buildings in the nation's Capital," violated the general conspiracy law. The second offense, a conspiracy to "kidnap Presidential adviser Henry Kissinger," also violated the federal kidnap law. The first offense carried a five-year sentence. The second could lead to life imprisonment.

But *after* its first indictments, on January 12, 1971, the grand jury continued to hear witnesses, and it issued a second indictment on April 30, in which it dropped the more serious charge, involving kidnapping.

Neither indictment had named Daniel Berrigan as a conspirator, despite Director Hoover's charges to the Senate subcommittee, and the second indictment even dropped his name from those mentioned as *"unindicted* co-conspirators."

The charging of persons with violations of federal laws is normally a serious procedure. The Department of Justice has hundreds of attorneys on its staff. It is an arm of the President, charged with seeing that federal laws are obeyed. One would expect it to act with respect for the law it upholds.

The FBI, part of the Department of Justice, would also be expected to act in a law-abiding manner. The FBI, as part of the Department of Justice, was, by law, supposed to be under the control of the head of the department, the Attorney General. But in this case, from beginning to end, these roles had been reversed. The Department of Justice was working for the FBI. Only in this way could all the strange things about the case, noticed by attorneys familiar with usual government practices in bringing indictments, be explained.

In the first place, Director Hoover had announced the charges to the public while the case was still being investigated. If any ordinary agent of the FBI had done such a thing, Hoover would have fired him immediately. Then, when the charges were finally made, two months later, they differed from those Hoover had announced. Then, after the indictments were handed down, the grand jury had continued digging for facts.

This could only mean one thing. The original January 12 indictment had been drawn up very hastily, before the government really had enough facts to decide that the Berrigans could be charged with anything. That was why the grand jury had been kept investigating. This was confirmed by the second indictment which, after three more months of investigation, was weaker than the first.

In *The FBI and the Berrigans,* Nelson and Ostrow quote an unnamed Justice Department official as admitting that if Hoover had not accused the Berrigans before the Senate subcommittee, the kidnap-bombing case most likely would not have been brought. It was possible, the official thought, that Hoover had made the matter public in order to force the Justice Department to prosecute the Berrigans.

Did Director Hoover have anything to go on when he made his accusations in November? What information did the FBI have about the jailed Berrigans when he appeared before the Senate subcommittee?

The source of the accusations was revealed six months later when, on April 30, the second indictment was issued. Attached to the indictment were two letters, between two of the defendants. One was from Sister Elizabeth McAlister to Philip Berrigan. The other was a reply from Father Berrigan to Sister Elizabeth.

Sister Elizabeth's letter was written on August 18, shortly after Daniel Berrigan was captured. In it, she tried to reassure Philip Berrigan that all was not lost and that the movement would continue. As evidence that his friends on the outside were continuing their activities, she wrote that "Eq [Eqbad

Ahmad] called us up to Conn. last night along with Bill Davidon. . . . Eq outlined a plan for an action which would say—escalated seriousness—& we discussed pros and cons for several hours. It needs much more thought & careful selection of personnel. To kidnap—in our terminology make a citizen's arrest of—someone like Henry Kissinger. Him because of his influence as policy maker and yet sans Cabinet status, he would therefore be not be as much protected as one of the bigger wigs. . . . To issue a set of demands, e.g., cessation of the use of B-52s over N. Vietnam, Laos, Cambodia, & release of political prisoners. Hold him for about a week during which time big wigs of the liberal ilk would be brought to him—also kidnapped if necessary (which for the most part it would be)—& hold a trial or grand jury affair out of which an indictment would be brought.

"There is no pretense of these demands being met & he would be released after this time with a word that we're nonviolent as opposed to you who would let a man be killed—one of your own—so that you can go on killing.

"The liberals would also be released as would a film of the whole proceedings in which, hopefully, he would be far more honest that he is on his own territory . . ."

The reply from Philip Berrigan warned that kidnapping could lead to murder. He also thought that the plan was grandiose, since kidnapping Kissinger and the liberal jury would require dozens of people. "Nonetheless," he wrote, "I like the plan and am just trying to weave elements of modesty into it. Why not coordinate it with the one against capital utilities? . . . To disrupt them and then grab the Brain Child [Kissinger]—This would be escalation enough.

"This comes off the top of my head. Why not grab the Brain Child, treat him decently, but tell him nothing of his fate—or tell him his fate hinges on release of pol. people or cessation of air strikes in Laos. Then have batteries of movement people—Brain Child blindfolded—engage him on policy.

"After he had been taught (the consideration of his safety

will make him more and more human in his answers) get it filmed and recorded. One thing should be implanted in that pea brain—that respectable murderers like himself are no longer inviolable. (This should be done just before release.) And that if he doesn't work to humanize policy, the likes of him will be killed by less scrupulous people.

"Finally, that political prisoners are the best guarantees of his sweet skin's safety and that he better get them out of jail.

"Taken along these lines you have both a material and personal confrontation with the warmakers. The trick to pull off is to hit them very, very hard without giving them violence to react to, or justify themselves with. . . .

"I would sic Eq on it immediately, but tie it in with the D.C. fiasco, and keep his imagination under ropes. If the investment in our best people is excessive, and if they're caught —there'd be a massive manhunt—it would mean life. And this is a factor to be considered."

These letters, on their face, sounded damning. But it remained to be seen if they revealed a real plot or were merely the idle thoughts of a lonely man in jail and of a woman wanting to keep his spirits up. This would be revealed at the trial, a year later.

The way these letters came into the possession of the Department of Justice also came out during the trial.

Among the dozens of witnesses the FBI had rounded up in the early months of 1971, as the Harrisburg grand jury continued its investigation after the first indictment, were a number of students and faculty members at Bucknell University, in Lewisburg, Pennsylvania.

Lewisburg is also the site of the federal penitentiary where Father Philip was held from the time of his capture, on April 21, 1970, until late in August, when he joined his brother at Danbury Prison in Connecticut.

At the trial, the main witness for the prosecution was a thirty-two-year-old man named Boyd F. Douglas, Jr. Boyd

Douglas had smuggled letters in and out of Lewisburg Penitentiary for Philip Berrigan. He was able to do this because he
was a fellow prisoner who was allowed to attend Bucknell
University during the day as part of a new federal program
allowing some prisoners to obtain higher education.

He had started acting as a courier in May, a month after
Philip Berrigan entered the penitentiary, when one of his
professors at Bucknell, Richard Drinnon, gave him a message
for the priest.

In June, a prison guard found a smuggled letter inside
a magazine in Douglas's cell. Shortly thereafter, he was con-
tacted by Field Agent Delmar Mayfield of the FBI and employed as a paid informer.

Douglas's usual method of smuggling a letter was to have
a girl friend copy it in one of the Bucknell student notebooks
he carried with him, with a heading and lead paragraph to
make it look like an essay. But unknown to Berrigan or anyone else in the peace movement, Douglas was Xeroxing the
originals of the letters and passing them on to Agent Mayfield.

At the trial, Boyd Douglas spent more than a week on the
witness stand answering the prosecutor's questions. Douglas
and Philip Berrigan had become friends. In addition to acting
as a courier, Douglas had given Berrigan an ROTC manual
on explosives supplied by Agent Mayfield, in hopes of trapping
the priest into committing an illegal act. Freely moving in and
out of jail, Douglas met many other people in the peace movement. He gave unsupported testimony about their kidnapping
and bombing plans. This was the only evidence the government had to support the two letters.

But Douglas's record, and the testimony of many of the
other witnesses who knew him, revealed that he was a ha-
bitual liar. Douglas's own father said that he never could believe what his son said. Douglas had told Berrigan and other
peace movement people that he had been jailed for war resistance. In fact, he was in jail for passing bad checks and for
threatening a bank auditor with a gun.

Douglas had lied in one way or another to everyone who knew him at Bucknell. He had told several girls he had asked to marry him that he was dying of cancer. He talked one of these girls into attending a war-protest meeting, then reported her to the FBI as a campus radical.

He had received about $9,000 from the FBI for his services; $1,500 for information leading to arrest of Rochester draft-board evaders; and a $200 reward for the capture of Daniel Berrigan, whose presence on Block Island was revealed in one of the smuggled letters. The FBI paid him to telephone Sister Elizabeth and other members of the movement and to tape-record their conversations. Then he collected money from Professor Drinnon for his expenses in making these same telephone calls. On October 3, 1970, a month before Director Hoover made his accusations to the Senate subcommittee, Douglas had written to Agent Mayfield asking for $50,000 tax free "to help the Government obtain enough evidence to prosecute these people concerned."

Sister Elizabeth and Father Philip were in love. They were separated, and Boyd Douglas was the only link between them. Douglas telephoned Sister Elizabeth in New York to tell her what Philip was thinking, and then told Philip, in prison, what Elizabeth was thinking. Much of their communication was carried on in this way, rather than by the smuggled letters, and Douglas was in a position to mislead both of them.

Philip Berrigan told Jack Nelson and Ronald Ostrow that Douglas gave him "an exaggerated version of the consciousness of those outside—he lied to me as to their thinking, aspirations, present involvements. By the same token, he lied about my consciousness, giving my friends a distorted picture of what I was thinking. He adopted a triple role, informer, provocateur and entrapper—out of these roles came the plot which he presented to the FBI."

Sixty-four government witnesses appeared at the trial, including twenty-one FBI agents and nine policemen, but only

Boyd Douglas knew anything about the kidnap-bomb plot. If there was more to it than what Sister Elizabeth and Father Philip had written in the two smuggled letters, only Boyd Douglas could say.

He gave a lot of testimony about plans to buy explosives and visits to underground tunnels in Washington, but no one else corroborated any of this. The jury did not believe him, for when the trial was over, the only result was that of all the defendants only Philip Berrigan and Sister Elizabeth McAlister were found guilty. And they were found guilty only of smuggling letters.

It was hard to escape the conclusion that a great deal of government money and effort had been wasted in trying to make trouble for a couple of unconventional priests who opposed the war in Vietnam.

The trial of Philip Berrigan and the other members of the "Harrisburg Seven" followed a pattern used by the government in other cases against opponents of the war. The government, and J. Edgar Hoover, had been stung by the popularity of the Berrigans' acts of vandalism. The Nixon administration was deeply disturbed by the demonstrations of veterans of the unpopular war, fearing that their military experience would give their opinions a respect beyond that afforded other antiwar activists.

In the Harrisburg case, the government had one agent, Boyd Douglas, encouraging Philip Berrigan to break the law. When, the following year, it indicted seven members of the Vietnam Veterans Against the War (VVAW) for plotting to disrupt the Republican National Convention by starting fires in Miami and terrorizing the police, the government produced six informers who had posed as members of the group. The informers, five of whom worked for the FBI and one of whom was a member of the Miami police, used their government funds to achieve important positions in the veterans group, and one offered to help it buy machine guns.

The Justice Department's Internal Security Division,

which assisted in the prosecution of both this case and the Berrigan one, displayed a low regard for the defendants' constitutional rights. During the first day of the veterans' trial, it was revealed that two FBI agents had been found with wiretapping and bugging equipment in a broom closet adjoining the room that the court had assigned to the veterans' defense counsel. And one of the informers, a close friend and associate of one of the defendants, had sat in on many of the meetings at which defense lawyers had discussed strategy.

The jury, finding the informers a shabby lot, acquitted the defendants after less than four hours of deliberation. The *New York Times* called this a "deserved rebuke for the Administration in its efforts to prosecute antiwar activists by infiltrating their ranks with undercover agents and provocateurs. . . .

"Particularly disturbing were repeated indications at the trial that the people the Government had planted inside the antiwar group sought to incite violence of precisely the kind the Government was professedly trying to stop."

In saddling the American people with an unjust war made, many believed, in defiance of the Constitution, the government aroused opposition that it sought to suppress by employing still more injustice. This pattern of suppression following injustice was one very familiar to the generation that came of age in 1776.

In proportion as the nation's statecraft is increasingly devoted to the gainful pursuit of international intrigue, it will necessarily take on a more furtive character, and will conduct a larger proportion of its ordinary work by night and cloud. —THORSTEIN VEBLEN, *Absentee Ownership*, 1923

The Birth of the CIA

The CIA threatens Americans and their constitutional rights in a different manner from the FBI.

To understand this, we must return to the intentions of the nation's founders as expressed in the Constitution. The fundamental idea of the Revolution was that government could not do whatever it wanted. Limits were put on the new government in two ways. In the first place, it was absolutely forbidden to do certain things, such as issue bills of attainder—laws designed to punish certain persons—or to issue search warrants without oath as to probable cause and without naming the object of the search.

In the second place, the entire structure of government was so designed that it was difficult for it to exceed these limits. Those who wrote the Constitution knew that mere prohibitions were not enough to ensure liberty. Experience had proven that a Bill of Rights "failed when it was most needed," Madison had written to Jefferson in 1788.

Knowing that no mere guarantee of liberty could withstand the power of government, the power itself was made difficult to exercise. The government was designed like a watch. No one part could operate without the others.

First of all, power was divided between the state governments and the nation. Then the power of the national government was divided among three branches, each of which would jealously watch the other two. The Congress was given the powers to make laws and to raise money and control its spending (the power of the purse). The President was given the power to execute the laws written by Congress and to represent the nation among other nations. The courts were independent of the other two branches and were given the right, as asserted by Chief Justice John Marshall of the Supreme Court, to decide on the constitutionality of acts and actions of Congress and the President.

To some extent, the FBI and the CIA represent ways in which our government both oversteps specific prohibitions and threatens the delicately balanced structure of our government. The FBI threatens specific prohibitions, such as the right to be let alone. It threatens the structure when it is used by Presidents—as it has been—to snoop on congressmen and weaken their opposition.

The CIA threatens our right to be let alone since it has, in violation of its charter, engaged in spying on Americans within the United States.

But the main threat of the FBI has been against the Bill of Rights, and the main threat of the CIA has been against the structure of our government.

An organ of the Executive branch of government—the President—the CIA is not properly accountable to the Congress of the people. It has therefore become one of the means by which modern Presidents have become excessively powerful, encroaching on the legislature.

The CIA is a child of the post–World War II world. Its

roots go back to the beginnings of that war, when the surprise attack on Pearl Harbor and an astounding lack of information on the Japanese enemy impressed President Roosevelt with the need for better intelligence. The problem was not felt to reflect so much on the ability of the military and State Department intelligence services to get enough information, but on putting it together and presenting it to the President and other decision makers in a usable form.

To remedy this, President Roosevelt named Colonel William J. Donovan, a prominent lawyer who had led the famous "Fighting 69th" regiment in World War I, as coordinator of information. Donovan found the task of coordinating information from the rival intelligence services difficult. His new organization soon became the Office of Strategic Services (OSS), an organization with a different mission. This was *covert operations,* secret activities behind enemy lines.

Secret operations have always been part of warfare. During the Civil War, for example, the Union forces had sent a team of men in civilian clothes behind rebel lines to steal a railroad train; and the Confederates had sent saboteurs north to set fire to hotels and encourage riots.

But the OSS was the first organization set up especially to conduct this kind of warfare. Thousands of operators were slipped into occupied Europe to assist guerrilla units and to carry out sabotage operations. The persons engaged in such missions, unlike regular soldiers, operated on their own, outside military discipline. Treading enemy territory in defiance of its laws, they had to act like bandits to survive. No deed, whether robbery, burglary, kidnapping, or murder, was forbidden in pursuit of their objectives.

Such activities were justified in a war against a ruthless enemy who also showed no scruples; but as soon as the war ended, the OSS was disbanded.

The idea of a centralized intelligence authority, however, persisted, fostered by General Donovan and other former OSS officials like Allen Dulles, who had been the chief American spy in Switzerland. In 1947, then, at the same time that the Defense Department was formed out of the combined Departments of War, Navy, and Air, the CIA was born.

Unlike the FBI, the CIA was legislated into existence. This means that a law was passed defining its powers. And as Congress discussed the new legislation, its concern centered, as it had forty years earlier in the case of the FBI, on the dread that the new agency would spy on Americans. "This is a very great departure from what we have had in the past in America," Congressman Clarence J. Brown of Ohio said. The United States ought to have good foreign intelligence, he added, but he didn't want to allow any "President . . . to have a Gestapo of his own if he wants to have it."

Secretary of the Navy James Forrestal, a spokesman for the administration, replied that the purposes of the CIA were "limited definitely to purposes outside of this country, except the collation of information gathered by government agencies." Domestic operations, Forrestal explained, were the province of the FBI.

Dr. Vannevar Bush, another administration spokesman, told the committee, "The bill provides clearly that it is concerned with intelligence outside of this country."

Despite these assurances, the legislature insisted on writing into the law a clause forbidding the agency to have any "police, subpoena, law-enforcement powers, or any internal security functions."

When the purpose of the new agency was described by various officials, it was pictured, as David Wise, one of the authors of the book *The Invisible Government,* has said, as "largely a collection of researchers clipping copies of Pravda and poring over Soviet railroad timetables." The idea was very close to that which President Roosevelt had in mind when he made Donovan coordinator of information in 1941. The emphasis was on putting together information collected by others:

by the intelligence services of the Defense and State departments. The hearings and debates do not suggest that Congress intended the CIA to engage in covert operations; but whether they realized it or not, the door was left open to them, and to almost any other sort of activity, by a catch-all provision that said the agency was "to perform such other functions and duties related to intelligence affecting the national security as the National Security Council may from time to time direct."

It was envisaged that the newly formed National Security Council, consisting of the President, vice-president, secretaries of state and defense, and other high officials, would keep close tabs on the CIA, which was to report to them. And also, of course, that congressional committees would exercise oversight, as they did over other government agencies.

For God shall bring every work into judgement, with every secret thing, whether it be good, or whether it be evil. —ECCLESIASTES 12:13

The First Time Our Government Was Caught Lying

Whatever the expectations of Congress regarding the purposes of the CIA, the new agency was soon involved in a whole series of secret operations abroad. Under Vice-President Truman, it began a series of small invasions of Albania aimed at the overthrow of the communist leadership. These resulted in nothing more than the capture of the invaders. It also supervised a force of 11,000 Chinese Nationalist troops in Burma and parachuted spies into mainland China and the Ukraine, most of whom were never heard of again.

These were all small operations involving relatively few Americans who, in the tough underground world of international intrigue, could be considered expendable. If they were caught, the U.S. government could deny knowing anything about them. It could, as was the custom in such cases, avoid embarrassment by refusing to help them.

But, like other bureaucracies, the CIA grew, and the National Security Council planned bigger and bigger things for it. Secret operations greatly expanded under President Eisenhower, who appointed John Foster Dulles secretary of state and his brother, Allen, head of the CIA (Director of Central Intelligence, DCI). The Dulles brothers sent their friend Kermit Roosevelt (son of former President Theodore Roosevelt) to Iran to engineer the overthrow of leftist Premier Mossadegh and secretly sent piloted combat aircraft and arms to Guatemala to overthrow President Arbenz. They provided the same sort of assistance in an unsuccessful effort to oust President Sukarno from Indonesia.

It is possible that the National Security Council did not give much thought to all the consequences of what it was doing as secret operations gradually became bigger—involving more people and more equipment. The NSC may have thought that the only difference between sending a few men to Albania and a hundred men, with B-26 bombers, to Guatemala was that the second operation, being bigger, had more chance of success.

But as operations became bigger, they became harder to conceal. An American in dungarees, found with false papers in the hills outside Tirana, could be disowned in Washington without arousing suspicion. Who would believe a spokesman for the communist government of Albania against the U.S. State Department?

Each operation required lies. The government lied about Guatemala, denying it had played any role in Arbenz's overthrow. Both President Eisenhower and Secretary of State Dulles lied about Indonesia. When Allen Pope, an American pilot working for the CIA, was captured, it was claimed that he was a freelance "soldier of fortune." There were some who doubted the government's stories, but there was no real proof either way, and in the minds of most Americans, the government was given the benefit of the doubt.

But what would happen if the United States was caught lying and had to admit it?

On Tuesday, May 3, 1960, some attentive American newspaper readers might have noticed a small news item saying that an American air base in Turkey reported the loss of a weather research plane based at Icirlik. The plane, the story said, had been lost near the Persian border.

Two days later, on May 5, Soviet Premier Nikita Khrushchev was speaking at a state occasion in the Great Hall of the Kremlin. Near the end of his three-and-a-half-hour speech, he announced that on May 1, the Soviet's most important holiday, "at 0536 hours, Moscow time, an American plane flew over our frontier and continued its flight into the interior of the Soviet land." The plane, he added, was shot down. He looked up at U.S. Ambassador Llewellyn Thompson and asked, "What is this, May Day greetings?"

Khrushchev wondered, he said, if by this "aggressive act," certain people in the United States were trying to torpedo a summit meeting between himself and President Eisenhower, scheduled to begin on May 16.

It was 1:30 in the afternoon in Moscow when Khrushchev made this announcement. It was 6:30 in the morning, Washington time.

That morning, as they waited for further statements from their government, all American newsmen could do was reexamine the original report that no one had noticed two days before.

In their book *The U-2 Affair,* authors David Wise and Thomas Ross report that the story had been picked up at the Icirlik air base, near the town of Adana, by Yusuf Ayhan, a local reporter who earned extra money as a part-time stringer correspondent for a newspaper in Istanbul. From there it had been sent to one of the big American news services in New York.

"An American plane of the U-2 meteorological reconnaissance type, which is well known for its excellent performance, and was based at Icirlik near Adana," Ayhan's story read, "was reported missing on Sunday. The U-2 plane, which flies at an altitude of over 10,000 meters [33,000 feet] . . . to investigate the reasons behind the changes in weather conditions, had sent its last message on Sunday, when the pilot reported a breakdown of his oxygen equipment. No further news was received from the plane after that."

Yusuf Ayhan knew that the border between Turkey and Persia (Iran), where the plane was reported down, was also close to the border of Soviet Armenia. He asked if it was possible that the plane had been shot down by Russian fighters.

This was denied. The Icirlik base gave him a press bulletin that, he wrote, "said it was possible that the plane in question made a false landing in the vicinity of Lake Van [in eastern Turkey]. It is reported that other planes which took off from Tripoli to search for the missing plane have failed to garner any information."

Was this "U-2 meteorological reconnaissance type" plane the one that the Russians were claiming to have shot down over Russia? The air force said it had gone down in eastern Turkey. Khrushchev said the plane "flew over our frontier and continued its flight into the interior of the Soviet land."

The news service story said that the pilot had reported "a breakdown of his oxygen equipment." This sounded as if the aircraft, out of control because its pilot had blacked out, may have accidentally strayed across the Soviet border. From the description, it was an innocent plane engaged in scientific research.

If the Russians had indeed shot it down, they had attacked an unarmed plane that was out of control due to an accident. It sounded as if the Russians were up to another of their dirty tricks.

Many reporters, like most American citizens, were angry

at this. *An American plane shot down, by the Russians.* They wanted more information. At the least the Russians ought to be warned that they couldn't just go shooting down unarmed American research planes whenever they felt like it.

That Thursday, after the Khrushchev speech, the U.S. government remained silent until a few minutes after noon. Then, five and a half hours after the Khrushchev announcement, President Eisenhower's press secretary, James Hagerty, told waiting reporters that the President had ordered a complete inquiry into the matter, the results of which would be made public by the National Aeronautics and Space Administration (NASA) and the Department of State.

About half an hour later, the State Department declared that it had been informed by NASA that, "as announced on May 3, an unarmed plane, a U-2 weather research plane based at Adana, Turkey, piloted by a civilian, has been missing since May 1. During the flight of this plane, the pilot reported difficulty with his oxygen equipment. Mr. Khrushchev announced that a U.S. plane has been shot down on that date. It may be that this is the missing plane. It is entirely possible that having a failure in the oxygen equipment, which could result in the pilot losing consciousness, the plane continued on automatic pilot for a considerable distance and accidentally violated Soviet air space. The United States is taking this matter up with the Soviet government, with particular reference to the fate of the pilot."

In *The U-2 Affair,* Wise and Ross tell how the State Department spokesman, Lincoln White, answered questions after reading the statement:

Q. Linc, how do you know the plane was having difficulty?
A. He reported it.
Q. He reported it by radio?
A. That is right.
Q. At what time did he give his position?

A. In the Lake Van area.

Q. Was his course such at this time that if continued it might have taken him over to the Soviet Union?

A. I don't have any of those details.

Searching for more details, the newsmen went over to the NASA office, where another press briefing began at half past one. The reporters were not disappointed.

The U-2 plane, the NASA spokesman explained, had been on a triangular course. From Adana northeast to Lake Van, from Lake Van northwest to Trebizond, from Trebizond southwest to Antalya, then east back to Adana. It was a 1,400-mile trip, scheduled to last 3 hours and 45 minutes. The pilot was last heard from by emergency radio on a northeasterly course, while over Lake Van but before making the turn to the northwest. This course, if continued, would obviously have taken him over the Soviet border.

The pilot, like all U-2 pilots, was employed by Lockheed. The NASA spokesman, quoting from published information, said that the plane could fly for as long as four hours at altitudes up to 55,000 feet. The U-2's instruments would permit "more precise information about clear air turbulence, convective clouds, wind shear, the jet stream and . . . typhoons . . . cosmic rays . . . ozone and water vapor." The reporters were given a long list of technical equipment carried by the U-2 to measure temperature, humidity, and air speed.

A reporter asked why the plane had been flying so close to the border of the Soviet Union. The answer was that the weather-research program was world-wide.

Did the U-2 carry air force cameras?

Yes, the NASA spokesman said, but he explained that "they are not reconnaissance cameras. They are cameras to take cloud cover pictures." The U-2 program, he added, had never been a classified secret.

The NASA spokesman, Walter T. Bonney, explained that

planes were still searching the Lake Van area in what could be a wasted effort. "If the Soviets would identify the U-2 as the plane they shot down," he added, "we would quit looking for it."

In the Senate, there was anger over the way the Russians had viciously shot down an unarmed weather-research plane as its pilot fought to keep conscious while his oxygen supply dwindled. Senator Styles Bridges of New Hampshire thought that Eisenhower should refuse to go to the summit conference in Paris until he had an explanation from the Soviets of their action.

Senator Mike Mansfield of Montana said that it wasn't nice for the Russians to "shoot first and complain later." Millions of Americans were thinking the same thing.

Later that afternoon, Press Secretary Hagerty told reporters that the inquiry ordered by the President had been completed. One reporter asked if the President was aware of the NASA weather-research flights. Hagerty could not answer this.

At five mintes to six, the Lockheed Aircraft Corporation in Burbank, California, gave out the name of the missing pilot of the U-2: Francis Gary Powers. When Lockheed officials were asked for more information on the U-2, they replied that "information about it was highly classified." They referred newsmen to NASA (whose spokesman, just a few hours before, had said that the U-2 program had never been classified).

The following day, Friday, May 6, at 12:35 P.M., State Department spokesman Lincoln White was asked by a reporter if there had been any change in orders to U.S. planes operating near the Soviet border. As authors David Wise and Thomas Ross reported in their very good book *The U-2 Affair,* Lincoln White replied that there was no change to be made. "This gentleman informed us that he was having difficulty with his oxygen equipment," White said. "Now, our assumption is that the man blacked out. There has been absolutely no—N-O—no

★ **100**

deliberate attempt to violate Soviet air space. There never has been."

In Moscow, earlier that same morning, Soviet Foreign Minister Andrei Gromyko had made fun of the story that the U-2 pilot had blacked out. He asked, Had all the pilots of all the planes that had been shot down over the years, flying over the Soviet border, also blacked out? "Are they suggesting that the crews of American planes sent to intrude into the territory of the USSR lose consciousness the minute they cross the Soviet border? This is really a new problem for medicine!"

Asked about Gromyko's statement, White said that he had no comment, "except to say that this is the information which we have, and it is ridiculous to say we are trying to kid the world about this."

N-O deliberate attempt to violate Soviet air space. This was an official spokesman for the U.S. government speaking. His first name was Lincoln, after Abraham Lincoln, who said, "Honesty is the best policy."

The State Department, through Lincoln White, had answered Gromyko's charge that the U-2 pilot had not been unconscious when he crossed the Soviet border. Now Khrushchev would give his answer to the State Department.

On Saturday, the day after Lincoln White said that it was ridiculous that the United States was trying to kid the world, Khrushchev announced that the pilot of the U-2 was alive and healthy and in Soviet hands. He had not mentioned this on Thursday, he explained, in order to see what lies the Americans would tell.

The Americans had released the oxygen-trouble stories, he said, because they had assumed that if the plane was shot down, the pilot "most probably perished, too. So there will be nobody to ask how everything actually happened, there will be no way to check what sort of plane it was and what instruments it carried."

Khrushchev said that the pilot was in Moscow and that

Three months after being shot down over Sverdlovsk, U-2 pilot Francis Gary Powers stands in the dock in a Soviet courtroom to hear his sentence for espionage—ten years. To his left stands his attorney, Mikhail Grinev.

(*United Press International*)

he was a first lieutenant in the U.S. Air Force in which he served up to 1956, when he joined the Central Intelligence Agency.

"This was a real military reconnaissance aircraft . . . for collecting intelligence and among other things, for aerial photography. . . . The task of the plane was to cross the entire territory of the USSR from the Pamirs to the Kola Peninsula to get information on our country's military and industrial establishments . . ."

Khrushchev, back in the Great Hall of the Kremlin, displayed photographs that had been developed from the plane's film. "Here are photos of these airfields. Here are two white lines. They are lines of our fighters." He also showed photographs of petrol depots. "That is what 'air samples' American reconnaissance took," he added.

The pilot, Francis Powers, Khrushchev declared, had said that his mission was to fly from Peshawar, Pakistan, to Bodo, Norway, and that he believed his flight over Soviet territory was "meant for collecting information on Soviet guided missiles and radar stations."

It was one in the afternoon in Moscow when Khrushchev made these revelations; six in the morning in Washington. State Department spokesman Lincoln White, awakened by a telephone caller with the news, soon satisfied himself that Khrushchev was lying. Khrushchev had said that the U-2's mission would take it almost 4,000 miles from Pakistan to Norway. From what had been published about the U-2, he knew that its range was less than 2,000 miles.

White was soon to learn that he was wrong and that Khrushchev was telling the truth.

It took twelve hours for the American government to decide what to do. Khrushchev had very cleverly faked them out. He had set a trap for the Americans by not revealing how much he knew. He had hoped the Americans, thinking he had very little to go on, would lie and that is exactly what they had done.

At six o'clock Saturday afternoon, the good soldier, Lincoln White, was facing the American press with a new statement. "The Department has received the text of Mr. Khrushchev's further remarks about the unarmed plane which is reported to have been shot down in the Soviet Union," he began. "As a result of the inquiry ordered by the President, it has been established that insofar as the authorities in Washington are concerned, there was no authorization for any such flights as described by Mr. Khrushchev.

"Nevertheless, it appears that in endeavoring to obtain information now concealed behind the Iron Curtain, a flight over Soviet territory was probably undertaken by an unarmed civilian U-2 plane."

The statement went on to say that all countries practiced intelligence collection and that surveillance was needed to prevent surprise attacks.

Even this statement, as we shall see, was not the complete truth. One change was made a couple of days later, on Monday afternoon, when the State Department explained that the flights had been authorized by the President of the United States to protect the United States and the Free World against surprise attack, although he hadn't known of each particular mission.

The U.S. government, which had spent all day Thursday and Friday saying that the plane had accidentally strayed across the Soviet border had, on Saturday, changed its story to say that it had probably gone on purpose but was unauthorized. On Monday, it had changed its story again to admit that such flights were authorized by the President.

Americans who had grown up believing what their government said were stunned. Never before had they heard an official government spokesman say one thing on one day and then the opposite the next day.

There were more lies. What the government said was a "weather research" plane was a spy plane. The government said the plane was based in Icirlik and it was based in Peshawar. Nor was it, even now, telling the entire truth. It kept referring to the U-2 as a "civilian" aircraft when in fact it had been purchased by the U.S. Air Force and was being operated by the Central Intelligence Agency. It kept referring to the pilot as a civilian when in fact he was a CIA employee.

Why had the government lied?

To answer this question, we must understand what the U-2 plane was doing over the Soviet Union. It was a remarkable aircraft, essentially a glider with a large jet engine. With its 80-foot wingspread and a special engine, the 40-foot-long plane could fly as high as 80,000 feet, 25,000 feet higher than its publicly announced ceiling. And it could glide long distances to save fuel, which increased its range far beyond what the world was told. It was equipped with a camera with a lens that could take very detailed pictures. From fourteen miles up, its pictures could distinguish a bathtub from a bridge table. It also carried equipment to pick up and record radar signals and other radio messages.

The U-2 plane presented the U.S. government with a tremendous temptation. The early 1950s were the years in which the menace of hydrogen bombs in intercontinental rockets began to be realized. These weapons increased the chances of surprise attack and, correspondingly, made everyone less secure. They made it more important than ever that countries know what their possible enemies were up to.

In 1955, President Eisenhower proposed to the Soviet Union that each country allow aerial surveillance of the other. When the Soviets turned the idea down, the United States decided to conduct this surveillance anyway, without the Soviet's permission, using the U-2 plane.

The spy overflights began during the summer of 1956 and continued for four years until Gary Powers was shot down over Sverdlovsk. During that time, the flights provided much valuable information. The U-2 flights lessened the risk of war by giving the United States confidence that the Soviet Union was not planning a surprise attack. This was, in fact, the justification for the flights given on Monday evening, when the government admitted they were authorized by President Eisenhower.

The benefits of the program were great. But they were illegal, since Russia had not given the United States permission to fly over its territory. The U.S. government would have been extremely unhappy if the Russians had similarly invaded its air space.

People are tempted to do illegal or immoral things all the time, from snitching cookies to robbing banks. All such deeds, when discovered, bring punishment. We have a choice, when caught, of admitting our guilt and taking our medicine or of lying and trying to escape punishment.

When a nation does something bad, the choice is not that clear-cut. In the first place, what is the "nation"? The nation of the United States is all 200 million Americans. But there was no way the 200 million Americans could have approved the U-2 flights. To approve them, they would have had to have known about them. Even though the Russians knew about the flights from their radar, President Eisenhower felt he could not tell the American public about them. He would have had to admit that the United States was breaking international law by violating Soviet air space. He would also have been hurting the Russians' pride by letting the world see that they could not (until May 1960) shoot down planes that flew over their country without their permission. So in this case, the "nation" was a small group in Washington, the President and some close advisers. The President was not so much deceiving the Soviets as his own people. He had to worry about what the American people would do if they found out.

In the second place, the U-2 flights involved other countries. Gary Powers' plane took off from Pakistan and was supposed to land in Norway. If the President admitted the flights, he would get those two countries in trouble with the Soviet Union. (We would not like it if we discovered that a Soviet spy plane used bases in Canada and Mexico.)

President Eisenhower seems to have been the only person knowledgeable about the flights who was concerned about deceiving the American people. When Khrushchev announced that the plane had been shot down, Eisenhower's instinct was to tell the truth, but it was already too late to be candid without disclosing that someone else in the U.S. government had lied.

This was because the lies had automatically been set in motion the minute the plane was missing, two days before the Khrushchev announcement. The Icirlik story picked up by Yusuf Ayhan had originated at CIA headquarters in Washington. This was all part of an elaborate "cover" plan worked out by the CIA in advance. Every spy has a cover to disguise his real purpose. The U-2 cover was that it was a NASA weather-research plane.

If there had been no cover story, the United States would not have been on record as having said anything about the plane before Khrushchev spoke on Tuesday. There would then have been no need, Tuesday afternoon, for the U.S. government to issue further lies, to protect its original cover story.

There was a cover story because the U-2 flights were run by the CIA as a spy program. The program included lots of "magic." The planes had been paid for by the air force, flown by air force pilots, and maintained by air force crews. The pilots and crews had been "sheep dipped." This means that they were apparently discharged from the air force and hired by Lockheed as civilians. In reality, they were not working for Lockheed at all, but for the CIA. Also, the Defense Department kept their records. At some future time, when the operation ended, they would rejoin the air force with the same promotions and pay as if they had never been out of the service.

Was Gary Powers a spy or wasn't he? He was put in civilian clothes in an unmarked plane. That sounds like a spy. But he was allowed to carry all sorts of personal identification including his driver's license and his Defense Department identification card—the last things any spy would have on him.

The basic trouble was that it was a big program that, because of secrecy, was known to very few. This limited the number of those who could advise the President on how things should be handled when they went wrong. Indeed, since those who knew about the program were those who had pushed for it and worked out its procedures, secrecy made the President a prisoner of those least qualified to give him sound advice. It was too big and too important to be run by spies.

The CIA covered the U-2 operation with layers of secrecy that confused other people in the government more than they did the Russians. Plenty of people in important positions, like Lincoln White in the State Department and Senator Styles Bridges, had no idea what was going on. Ultimately, the CIA's hocus-pocus resulted in a series of lies that damaged Americans' faith in their government.

This was a very serious matter. Freedom is a delicate principle. Our ability to live in harmony with one another, with a minimum of force or interference in our private lives, is based on our respect for law. This respect for law is based on our written Constitution and the government that gives it life.

Khrushchev called off the summit meeting, and Eisenhower promised to send no more planes over Russia. Gary Powers spent two years in Soviet prisons before he was released in exchange for an important Russian spy, KGB agent Rudolph Abel.

Would Americans, who learned their government had deceived them, ever trust it again? If they did not, could they be expected to obey it of their own free will? If an untrustworthy government had to resort to force to compel obedience, could it still be called a "government by the consent of the governed"?

In practicing deceit, the government embarked on a path that, by separating it from the people, would make it more dependent on force. Deceit is a first step on the road to tyranny.

A people who mean to be their own Governors must arm themselves with the power which knowledge gives.

— JAMES MADISON, letter to W. T. Barry, August 4, 1822

Magic in High Places

BACKGROUND

Late in 1960 and during the early months of 1961, thousands of Cubans were seen boarding planes in Florida and Louisiana. Soon stories were leaking out of Central America about mysterious military training camps in Guatemala and a fleet of B-26 aircraft in Nicaragua.

Alert reporters wrote stories that appeared in the Nation, *the* New York Times, *and other publications. When their stories got too specific and indicated that all this activity was aimed at an invasion of Cuba, editors, worried that they were possibly harming "national security," showed them to the President. Kennedy asked that the stories be suppressed.*

Then, on April 17, 1961, several thousand armed men landed at the Bay of Pigs, on the southern coast of Cuba. They were Cubans, returning to their homeland to topple the revolutionary government of Fidel Castro. Their plan was to hold the beach, proclaim a new "free" provisional government, and ask for American aid. But within a day they all were either killed or captured by the Cuban army.

President Eisenhower had gotten away with his denials of U.S. involvement in Guatemala and Indonesia, but President Kennedy was unable to conceal our connection with the Bay of Pigs. It was just too big an operation to be covert. He had to admit that the ships that carried the invaders to Cuba belonged to the CIA and that the agency had trained and armed the men, built the secret bases, and masterminded the entire operation.

After the invasion proved a disaster, Kennedy regretted that the newspapers had obeyed his request to suppress the stories of the invasion planning. He told an editor of the New York Times, *"If you had printed more about the operation you would have saved us from a colossal mistake."*

Too late, President Kennedy recognized one of the dangers of secrecy—that it could be used to prevent criticism.

Not all secrecy, of course, is dangerous. We want the government to keep some things secret, such as what we put on our income-tax forms. And we have already pointed out that the government is more at fault in releasing arrest files like Dale Menard's than in keeping them secret.

Secrecy is also important to all kinds of discussions since people will talk more freely—and more honestly—behind closed doors. (The convention at which the Constitution was written was secret.)

But secrecy in discussion is not the same as secrecy in action. Covert operations—that is, secret operations—were not supposed to be secret from everyone, of course. They were supposed to be known to the President, to the National Security Council, and to at least some committees of the Congress that represents the American people, who pay for everything and in whose name these actions are taken. But Congress knows almost nothing about them. "Fewer than a dozen mem-

bers of Congress have any idea how much money the CIA spends each year," said Representative Paul Findley of Illinois in 1973, "and probably none of them has much of an idea what the agency actually does with that money."

Keeping actions secret from Congress could have much worse results than just preventing criticism. It could unbalance the constitutional system of government. How could the machine designed by the founding fathers work if Congress did not know what the CIA was doing? How could the power of the President be checked? And if it was not checked?

After the Bay of Pigs, President Kennedy dismissed DCI Allen Dulles and tried to tighten his control over the agency. But Congress, and the American people, remained in the dark.

On December 7, 1963, when Secretary of Defense Robert McNamara was sent to Vietnam on a fact-finding mission by President Lyndon Johnson, things were not going well in that beleaguered country. The new government under General Minh, supported by the United States, was unpopular. The rebel Vietcong were making gains all over South Vietnam, despite the fact that in the past two years the number of American military "advisers" had increased tenfold, to 16,000.

The United States had actually been involved in Vietnam for nine years, and things never seemed to turn out as the Presidents' advisers expected. The reasons we took an interest in Vietnam—or anywhere in Indochina for that matter—have their roots in World War II, during which the French colonial grip on the region was loosened. While American agents of the OSS cooperated with Ho Chi Minh, the father of North Vietnam, and with his revolutionary Viet Minh, President Roosevelt dreamed that all colonialism would end after the war and that Indochina would eventually become independent.

Each President, from Franklin Roosevelt to Lyndon Johnson, was faced with things happening there that de-

manded immediate decisions. Whether he took action or post-
poned it, none clearly foresaw the consequences of his decisions; and each passed on to his successor unresolved chaos
that was somewhat worse than he had found it.

A sensible long-range policy could have been carried out
by a State Department whose officers possessed the courage to
fight for their convictions and who had the respect of successive Presidents and their secretaries of state. But for much of
this time we had a State Department demoralized by the same
kind of politically inspired loyalty inquisitions that troubled
William Remington. Many of those Foreign Service officers
best qualified to deal with Southeast Asia and China were
hounded from the government for having said what they
thought—that, for example, the Nationalist Chinese that we
backed were corrupt and destined for failure. Those who were
left meekly followed the wishes of politicians with short-term
goals.

The best of foreign services would have had difficulty in
making sense out of Vietnam. For a demoralized service, there
was no way to avoid disaster. Vietnam was a country with a
long history of division, internal conflict, and secret activity.
There were religious sects, tribal groups, bandits, mutual-aid
societies, guilds, villages, and ancient feuds. All this was ignored by successive policy makers who were unable to see the
country or its people as they really were. They tried to define
problems in American terms, which didn't apply to Vietnam.

In addition to all their misunderstandings of Vietnam,
America's policy makers feared that a communist victory there
would lead to communist victories elsewhere. Such "free world
allies" as Thailand and the Philippines were looked upon as
no more stable than upended dominoes. They would forsake
us, turning one after another to communism the way all the
dominoes in a row fall when one (Vietnam) is toppled.

President Johnson had been in office for just two weeks
when he sent McNamara to Vietnam on his fact-finding mission. There were a great many things Johnson didn't know

when the assassin's bullets that felled President Kennedy suddenly thrust him into the White House.

The assassination had created a break in the leadership of the government. There were people who had been serving President Kennedy, and who would continue to serve President Johnson, who knew more about what had been happening in Vietnam than President Johnson did. Johnson needed information, but he knew he had to be careful whom he consulted. Secretary McNamara did not get an accurate, balanced picture of what was going on in Vietnam. A special show was put on for him by military and civilian personnel who were getting their orders from the Pentagon.

These men, known as *briefers,* fed Secretary McNamara statistics and took him on a carefully planned tour that included glimpses of "combat devastated" villages and "close-in" combat that had been screened and planned in advance.

According to Colonel C. Fletcher Prouty, who at that time was the focal point officer between the Defense Department and the CIA, the production was managed by Prouty's associate, Marine General Victor H. Krulak of the Joint Chiefs of Staff. Krulak's office radioed messages to Saigon with instructions on what to show Secretary McNamara and sent statistics and reports to brief him. It even sent messages to Saigon that would be shown to McNamara and then radioed back to Washington as messages *from* McNamara. In other words, it was not only staging McNamara's trip and what he would see and hear, it was even writing his reactions to the trip. More important, it was writing the report he would submit to the President.

No doubt McNamara made some contributions to the report, but he had such a powerful, well-oiled machine helping him to see and understand and interpret and write about what was happening in Vietnam that it would be difficult for anyone to know what part of the report was the secretary's and what came from all the others masterminding special operations and "helping" him.

General Krulak worked through the night, while others wrote, typed, prepared tables of statistics and charts. The final, printed report, bound in black goatskin with the name of President Johnson engraved in gold, was then flown by helicopter to Andrews Air Force Base outside Washington and "placed aboard a military jet fighter for a nonstop, midair, refueled flight to Honolulu, where it was handed to Mr. McNamara and his staff." Thus the Secretary of Defense was returning to Washington from Saigon with a report written in Washington. Colonel Prouty explained that the secretary familiarized himself with the report on his way back to Washington.

When McNamara entered the White House with the report tucked under his arm, President Johnson would think that he was bringing him the latest and best information from Vietnam. Everything in the report had been written in Washington, and everything McNamara had seen and heard had been part of a script prepared by General Krulak's office.

(*New York Times* columnist Russell Baker later humorously suggested that the government didn't really send secretaries and congressmen to Vietnam at all, but to *Disneynam,* built outside Rockville, Maryland, by the creators of Disneyland. There, an actor played the part of South Vietnam's president and writers from defunct magazines wrote fake dispatches from Hanoi predicting victory unless Congress gave money for the war.)

The staging of the show also had included slipping copies of McNamara's report beforehand to a number of President Johnson's closest advisers. These were men, many with long associations with the CIA, who were familiar with the course of special operations in Vietnam and who believed it was necessary to continue and to expand them. If McNamara's report, based on their recommendations, would deceive the President, it also would deceive them. For the same "facts and figures" that blinded McNamara could blind anyone who *wished to believe them.* And such was their confidence in their power,

Secretary of Defense Robert McNamara with General William Westmoreland (*left*) and President Lyndon Johnson (*right*). The date is July 13, 1967. Almost four years after President Johnson had taken office and McNamara had gone to get the facts in Vietnam, the United States was preparing to send still more troops to Southeast Asia. No outside opinion on what is happening sways their councils.   (*United Press International*)

and in the armed might of their country, that they could not doubt that in any event they could change reality to conform with what they believed.

With McNamara chock full of "personally witnessed" facts and with so many of his advisers armed with the same report, President Johnson was being "briefed" in the White House in the same distorted manner that McNamara had been "briefed" in Vietnam. This briefing was to change the course of U.S. history, setting the nation on the path to the most disastrous war it ever fought.

What was really happening in South Vietnam was that the

★ 115

American-supported government and army were arousing the opposition of the people. The Vietcong continued to grow in strength not because they were coming down from the North and getting supplies from there. The Vietcong were mostly South Vietnamese people who hated the corrupt and unrepresentative government put over them by the Americans. As Green Beret Master Sergeant Donald Duncan reported after he left Vietnam, "The more often government troops passed through an area, the more surely it would become sympathetic to the Viet Cong."

This is not to say that North Vietnam was blameless. The Hanoi government was sending men and equipment into the South. But the briefing was written as if the North Vietnamese had started all the trouble. They were the "bad guys" and we were the "good guys." Actually, the United States had secretly started making trouble in the North before North Vietnam started making trouble in the South.

The President's briefing also mentioned that "1000–1500 Viet Cong cadres entered South Vietnam from Laos in the first nine months of 1963." It did not mention that for every organizer who came down from the North there were dozens of native South Vietnamese fighting the government, or that many of the guerrilla fighters were not communists at all. As Douglas Pike, a U.S. information officer with years of experience in Vietnam wrote, many were from the Cao Dai and Hoa Hoa religious sects and others represented "a scattering of minority group members, primarily ethnic Cambodians and montagnards; idealistic youth recruited from universities . . . representatives of farmer organizations . . . leaders of small political parties or groups . . . intellectuals who had broken with [the government of South Vietnam]; military deserters, refugees . . . from the Diem government."

The President's briefing not only did not mention how many different types of Vietnamese were fighting the South Vietnamese government, but it also did not mention how most South Vietnamese felt about American support.

It was written as if what was happening in South Vietnam was a struggle between the communist world, which was supporting the Vietcong, and the free world, which was supporting the South Vietnamese. In fact, it was a war for national independence.

If President Johnson had been exposed in December to a broad range of information and opinion, he would have had a chance to make a wise decision. Instead, the one-sided briefing recommending more covert operations and gloomily predicting that "more forceful" measures might be needed led him to encourage the very activity that was making the situation worse. The more American support he sent to South Vietnam, the more Vietcong he created.

In three years, Johnson raised the American presence from 16,000 troops to 550,000. When the Americans finally left, in 1973 during the Nixon administration, 43,000 had lost their lives, and there were more Vietcong than ever.

It has often been said that "knowledge is power." This is particularly true of *secret* knowledge. The CIA keeps all its papers locked up where no one else may see them without its permission. No one in the agency is allowed to tell anyone else what he is doing without permission. This applies not only when talking to people outside the agency, but also inside the agency itself. A CIA man on a project is told exactly who else in the agency may know what he is doing, and how much that other person may know. Thus, even those in the CIA itself do not know what others in the agency are doing.

Secrecy makes it possible for the CIA to prepare magical happenings like Secretary McNamara's trip to Vietnam in December 1963. Secrecy made magic possible. Secret operations extended the magic enormously until it shook the world.

The expansion of secret operations began when Presidents Truman and Eisenhower started the new policy of containment of communism. This meant stopping its spread to nations where its supporters were not in control.

To contain communism, the idea of counterinsurgency developed. Insurgency means revolution. It was thought that the communists would try to seize power in countries by starting revolutions. Of course, there were many reasons for starting revolutions besides communism. Many people in many parts of the world were badly treated by their governments and turned to armed revolt—insurgency—as a last resort when they could see no other hope for improving their lives.

But many Americans, as well as government officials charged with carrying out the policy of containment, came to fear all insurgents as communists and all grass-roots political changes as threatening to American interests. Insurgents in the Philippines, Brazil, and Thailand, for example, were opposed by counterinsurgents trained and assisted by the United States.

American counterinsurgency in Vietnam started in 1954, when the French colonial rulers left. In June of that year, while the French, Vietnamese, Russians, and Chinese were meeting in Geneva to arrange a peaceful future for Indochina, Edward G. Lansdale, a CIA operative under cover as an air force colonel, arrived in Saigon to begin secret operations against North Vietnam.

The Geneva agreement was made in July. The representatives of the two Vietnamese groups, communist and noncommunist, denounced it. The United States dissociated itself from the agreement, but agreed to follow its spirit. Three months after the agreement was signed, "Colonel" Lansdale's men were pouring junk into the oil used to lubricate Hanoi's buses, to ruin their engines, and printing fake leaflets to cause confusion. The group was soon training and supplying small groups of Vietnamese to sneak into North Vietnam to sabotage and spy. (Infiltration of South Vietnam from the North, according to Douglas Pike, did not begin until 1958 or 1959.)

The Geneva accord temporarily divided Vietnam into two parts for a two-year period. In 1956, a free election was to be held to decide the future of the country. President Eisenhower and his advisers decided that in any free election, the leader of the North Vietnamese, Ho Chi Minh, would get about 80 percent of the votes of the Vietnamese people. Since Ho was a communist, they decided secretly to prevent these elections from taking place by transforming South Vietnam from a temporary half of a country into a permanent country with a government of its own.

Meanwhile, American counterinsurgency was entering more and more countries. The programs were directed by a special staff of the National Security Council called the Special Group CI. When President Eisenhower left office, there were counterinsurgency operations in about seventeen countries. They were getting too large for the CIA to handle by itself, so the U.S. Army got into the act by sending special military missions, MAAGs, to train foreign troops in counterinsurgency. It also trained a new kind of soldier, the Special Force soldier, or Green Beret, actually to fight rebels, often under the operational control of the CIA.

When John Kennedy became President in 1961, he made General Maxwell Taylor, who had been working closely with the head of the CIA, Allen Dulles, his special military adviser. Later he promoted Taylor to the highest military post, chairman of the Joint Chiefs of Staff. One reason he did this was that General Taylor favored CI operations. The Green Berets were expanded, and they and more MAAGs were sent to even more countries.

With its MAAGs and Green Berets involved in secret operations, the army began confusing the old distinction between peace and war. American soldiers and civilians were now fighting in the jungles of Vietnam against local guerrilla forces and capturing Vietnamese Vietcong soldiers for purposes of interrogation. The CIA and the military in many places were training local troops, transporting them to sites of rebel activity, and even going into battle with Tibetan horsemen, Peruvian infantrymen, or Jordanian palace guards. Despite eyewitness reports that Americans were flying military aircraft and leading troops in combat, the Pentagon insisted that they only fired weapons in self-defense. They were fighting not under any declaration of war, not under the banner of the United Nations or under any treaty commitment, but purely under the authority of the President of the United States, as expressed through the Special Group CI. They were not, in the U.S. military tradition, proudly fighting under the Stars and Stripes. They were secret operators whose actions had to be lied about.

The Special Group CI gave the President a powerful weapon that kept expanding in size. It is difficult enough managing a growing operation that is visible. A growing operation that is secret is uncontrollable. The CIA was hidden inside Special Group CI like a secret within a secret. CIA men, working in army, air force, or navy uniforms, were known only to other CIA men. And the CIA, as it worked with more and more government departments—the Customs Bureau, for example, for the purpose of sneaking "black" secret cargoes into the country; the Post Office, which secretly opened and read private letters sent in and out of the United States—was able to plant its own people all through the government. With CIA operatives in unsuspected places, and with its own world-wide communications network and its control over the "briefing" of officials, the CIA was able to play a very important part in the making of foreign policy.

Secret operations were also used to deceive the American people. For example, on the night of August 4, 1965, the American people were told that two American destroyers, cruising in the Gulf of Tonkin off the east coast of North Vietnam, were attacked by North Vietnamese torpedo boats. Americans were outraged at this attack on their navy on the high seas; shortly thereafter, Congress passed the Gulf of Tonkin Resolution, authorizing the President to retaliate against North Vietnam.

The American people were told that the attacks by the torpedo boats were unprovoked. They were not told that earlier, on August 1 and August 2, Thai pilots working for the CIA and flying American T-28 jet planes, had bombed and strafed North Vietnamese villages. They were not told that CIA secret operatives had long been helping groups of South Vietnamese make guerrilla raids in North Vietnam; or that pilots working for Air America, an airline owned by the CIA, had been bombing North Vietnamese; or that since the night of July 30, South Vietnamese commandos, under American orders, had been raiding North Vietnamese islands in the Gulf of Tonkin, less than 150 miles from where the destroyers were sailing.

They were not told that the night before the U.S. destroyers were attacked, special, heavily armed U.S.-supplied PT boats, manned by South Vietnamese, bombarded the mouth of the Rhom River and a radar installation at Vinhson. This was all kept secret from the American people, as was the fact that, since February, the administration had been planning to widen the war. The Gulf of Tonkin Resolution had been written long in advance. The attack on American destroyers provoked by covert operations gave the President an excuse to present the resolution to Congress.

Through secrecy, the secret operations men of the Special Group CI were able to make things happen the way they wanted them to. The secret bombing raids by T-28 aircraft, and the secret PT boat and other over-the-border raids, were managed by the CI group in accordance with the recommendations Secretary McNamara had "brought back from Saigon."

The minds that planned the secret operations in Vietnam knew that they would provoke the North Vietnamese to do things that could be used as an excuse for the United States to take more action. In other words, secret operations gave them a way of manipulating the North Vietnamese as well as the American people.

As long as secret operations remain part of American

policy, it will be possible for other real-life dramas to be arranged in other parts of the world.

As *New York Times* reporter Neil Sheehan wrote in his introduction to *The Pentagon Papers,* which revealed some of the secret operations in Vietnam, "The . . . public world— Congress, the news media, the citizenry, even international opinion as a whole—are regarded from within the world of the government insider as elements to be influenced. . . . The papers also make clear the deep-felt need of the government insider for secrecy in order . . . to maintain a maximum ability to affect the public world."

Our involvement in Vietnam can certainly not be blamed on the CIA. But the agency changed the nature of the involvement. Without its covert operations, which obscured the real facts, events might not have gotten so badly out of hand. President Johnson was ultimately driven from office for engaging in a war contrary to the principles of the Constitution.

Justice is as strictly due between neighbor nations as between neighbor citizens. A highwayman is as much a robber when he plunders in a gang as when single; and a nation that makes an unjust war is only a great gang.

—BENJAMIN FRANKLIN

The Enemy We Made

BACKGROUND

Early in 1793, there arrived in Philadelphia, the capital of the four-year-old United States, a new minister plenipotentiary from France. The minister, Edmond Charles Genêt, as a representative of the revolutionary new French Republic, began recruiting Americans for an expedition against Spanish Florida and Louisiana. He also started raising money to arm American vessels and to issue commissions to American ships to act as privateers (pirates) against Britain. President Washington, horrified at this foreign interference in American affairs, told the French government to recall Genêt.

Today, other nations, even if they are as weak and insignificant as was America in 1793, resent meddling by outsiders.

We have forgotten this in making our counterinsurgency programs. Our training of police soldiers, our MAAGs and Green Berets, and the secret operations that accompany them, can arouse a dislike of the United States. Whatever benefits

★ **123**

we see, in terms of keeping order around the world, may in the long run prove small when measured against the cost in goodwill and trust.

As the British historian Arnold Toynbee noted in May 1970, America, to most Europeans, has come to seem the "most dangerous country in the world. . . .

"For the world as a whole, the CIA has now become the bogey that Communism has been for Americans. Wherever there is trouble, violence, suffering, tragedy, the rest of us are now quick to suspect the CIA had a hand in it. Our phobia about the CIA is, no doubt, as fantastically excessive as America's phobia about world Communism; but in this case, too, there is just enough convincing evidence to make the phobia genuine. In fact, the roles of America and Russia had been reversed in the world's eyes. Today America has become the world's nightmare."

Quebrada is a Spanish word for ravine. In the darkness of Saturday night, October 7, 1967, a band of eighteen men in sloppy fatigue clothes—loose khaki shirts and baggy pants—slowly entered the Quebrada del Churo.

It was a wild place with small, starved-looking trees, outcrops of granite, and tortuous paths carved down to the base rock by rainwater like some insane architect's idea of a stairway.

The eighteen men were tired and were trying to hide. The previous week they had been ambushed outside a small village and had lost three of their number. Their leader knew things were not going well. They had come to Bolivia to start a revolution, but the peasants did not trust them.

Their leader had much experience with revolutions. He had fought one in Cuba, starting in the eastern mountains with just such a small band as this. But there the peasants had helped the rebels, who were almost without exception Cubans like themselves. Here, it was different. Most of the men in the group were Cubans. They had much experience—four were generals in the Cuban army—but they did not speak or look like Bolivians, and the peasants looked upon them as enemies rather than friends.

So it was in this nowhere in eastern Bolivia, between the towering Andes and the steaming jungles of the Amazon, that it was the Bolivian army that knew where the rebels were rather than the rebels knowing where the army was. And looking up the craggy walls of the Quebrada at the stars, the leader felt, as he always did now, that they were being watched. They stopped at a small field of sweet potatoes, beside a pleasant little stream. There was a large fig tree, and as he dropped off to sleep under it the leader wondered about the loyalty of one of his men, Willi. On the whole their morale had been good, even though it seemed that the other band of rebels had been lost. But Willi, the leader suspected, might look for a chance to escape when they were attacked again.

Reports on exactly what happened the next day, Sunday, October 8, are fragmentary. By the time the rebels awakened that morning, they were surrounded by a company of 184 Bolivian rangers commanded by Captain Gary Prado who had been trained at Fort Bragg, North Carolina. At one in the afternoon, as the rebels tried to get out of the Quebrada, they were met with rifle fire. The rebels tried to go the other way, down to the river at the bottom of the Quebrada, but found themselves under attack again. During these two small battles they killed two of the rangers and wounded two others.

There was a period of silence, then, suddenly, explosions, wicked fragments of metal, the ground shaking, the growl of machine guns. A squad of rangers was coming up from the river. All the rebels could do was climb upward where machine guns were waiting for them.

The leader was hit in the leg. Another bullet broke the barrel of his rifle. Willi grabbed him and, holding his arm over his shoulder, helped him up the ravine. They clutched stems of thorns to pull themselves along, their hands were covered with blood. The leader was choking with an attack of asthma.

Four soldiers jumped up in front of them.

The leader said, "I am Che Guevara."

Ernesto "Che" Guevara was born in Argentina in 1928 into a middle-class family. He early developed a sympathy for poor people, who are plentiful in Latin America and whose misery Che saw at close hand during his extensive travels as a student.

Instead of taking up the practice of medicine, when he finished school in 1953, the twenty-five-year-old Ernesto Guevara went to Bolivia, where a new revolutionary government had just taken the tin mines from the foreign company that owned them. He was attracted to movements to improve the conditions of the poor but had no clear idea of how this should be done. All governments seemed more interested in helping themselves than helping the common people, yet how could people be helped without some sort of organization or government? From Bolivia, he went to Guatemala, where another revolutionary government under Dr. Jacobo Arbenz seemed willing to go further than the new Bolivian regime, since it was giving to the Indians valuable land that it had taken from the American-owned United Fruit Company.

At this time, Guevara was not a communist. What happened to the Arbenz government started his thoughts in that direction. The United Fruit Company prevailed on the Eisenhower government to overthrow the Arbenz regime so that its investment in Guatemala (and other Latin American countries that might be tempted to follow the example of Guatemala) would be protected.

This campaign against the government of an independent country was justified by the United States on the basis that communists were active in the Guatemalan government and that the communist governments of Eastern Europe were sending weapons to the Guatemalans. It was helped by the fact that there was growing disagreement among Arbenz's supporters over the aims of the revolution. The Guatemalan army wanted him to do more for the peasants, and the middle class was afraid of angering the United States.

On June 18, 1954, Guatemala was invaded by Guatemalan exiles trained and equipped by the CIA in Nicaragua and Honduras and supported by B-26 aircraft belonging to the CIA. As the Arbenz government collapsed, Guevara, for the first time, became a political activist. He rushed from one group of revolutionary (pro-Arbenz) students to another, urging them to arm the Indians to fight the invaders and protect their newly acquired land. But Arbenz's followers did not trust the Indians, and Guevara had to flee for safety to the Argentine embassy.

Guevara had been changed from an observer, sympathetic to the sufferings of the poor, into a revolutionary. As his first wife, Hilda Gadea, was to write, "It was Guatemala which finally convinced him of the necessity for armed struggle and for taking the initiative against imperialism." By "imperialism," Guevara meant the United States.

Up to this time, Guevara had shied away from political doctrines like Marxism, out of a belief that all bureaucracies, whether democratic or communist, were enemies of individual freedom. But his experience in Guatemala had taught him that individual revolutionaries or reformers were helpless against the power and organization of the United States. He therefore embraced communism, with its troublesome bureaucracy, as, he thought, the lesser of two evils.

In Mexico City, to which Guevara had gone from Guatemala, the young Argentinian avidly read Marx and other communist writers. Here, also, in the summer of 1955, he met Fidel Castro, who had just been exiled from Cuba for leading an unsuccessful coup against the dictator Fulgencio Batista.

The following year, Guevara sailed back to Cuba with Castro and eighty other men to begin the revolution that would bring them to power in 1959. Except for Fidel Castro himself, no one played a bigger part in the Cuban revolution than Che Guevara. It was he who was responsible for converting Castro to communism. With Castro, he plotted the course of the revolution after their victory. They came to rely more and more on the workers and peasants, as their leveling measures and taking of property drove away many of the middle-class liberals including Castro's own sister, Juanita, who had helped them to power.

Guevara wrote a book, *Guerrilla Warfare,* based on his experiences in fighting in Cuba. This book preached a new revolutionary doctrine that in many ways went against old, established communist ideas. Russian communists had long taught that revolutions must start among workers in the cities and could only be successful when the time was right, when capitalism was already falling apart due to its own problems.

Che Guevara's doctrine was seen by the CIA to be much more dangerous. He taught that the time was always right for revolution, as long as there were suffering people. He taught that the place to begin a revolution was among the peasants. The peasants were needed to support the revolution, by feeding and hiding the guerrilla fighters, joining their ranks, and supplying information on the location of government troops. The peasants were also the teachers of revolution, for it was by living among the poor peasants that the guerrilla fighters learned what had to be done to help them.

In this way, a small group of guerrilla fighters could gradually expand their numbers, taking over more and more of a country. According to this plan, the cities would fall at the end, when the entire countryside was in the rebels' hands and they were cut off.

This is pretty much the way the revolution had worked in Cuba, and Che Guevara thought it could be made to work anywhere in the world. This doctrine was not very different from that of the Chinese communists, as preached by Mao

Che Guevara on January 3, 1959, shortly after entering Havana at the victorious conclusion of the Cuban revolution.   (*United Press International*)

Tse-tung, but it had been worked out by Che and Castro on their own, with little knowledge of the way the Chinese had fought their revolution.

(Guevara's book, *Guerrilla Warfare,* was translated into many languages and inspired guerrilla fighters all over the world. It was read by the Vietcong in Vietnam, who often seemed to be following its teaching, and also by the Special Forces of the U.S. Army. The Green Berets, until they learned the common people resented them as foreigners, thought that they could do the same thing Che did—raise up armies among the South Vietnamese to fight as guerrillas against the guerrilla Vietcong. They also used it as a way of figuring out how the enemy operated.)

As Cuba became more deeply involved with the Soviet

Union as a source of outside support to keep the revolution in Cuba going, Guevara became more and more disillusioned. By 1964, he had come to see that the Soviet Union and other European communist nations were as imperialistic as the United States and its European allies, and he was preaching that all the countries of people whose skin was dark had to work together against the white imperialists. He had invented a new idea: the Third World, composed of all the poor countries of the southern part of the globe that were forced to sell raw materials to rich countries at low prices.

Guerrilla wars kept flaring up in one of these countries after another. South of the border, there were small rebel groups operating in Guatemala, Colombia, Venezuela, and Peru. More and more the United States was seeing Guevara as the chief planner of revolution. And Guevara, who was known to practice what he preached, was reported to be in the Congo in 1965, when fighting broke out against the Mobutu regime.

Then on March 23, 1967, there was a report of a clash between government troops and a small band of guerrillas near the Nancahuazú River in central Bolivia just east of the Andes. The following month, their camp was overrun. One of the things that was captured was a photograph of a partly bald, gray-haired man with glasses. The photo looked like Guevara, and some fingerprints on some of the captured papers seemed to match his.

The CIA, which had been out to get Guevara ever since he had left Cuba in 1965 with his talk of starting two or three more Vietnams, immediately sent some men to the scene to verify that Guevara was really the leader of these guerrillas. They had thick folders of pictures of Guevara and other information about him, and they interviewed peasants who had seen the fighters. Satisfied that Guevara was indeed in Bolivia, the CIA went into action.

Santa Cruz, in the heart of the rebel area, became a staging area for military shipments, and a Green Beret detachment was flown in from Canal Zone, Panama. While they set up camp at nearby La Esmeralda to train Bolivian troops in fighting guerrillas, three CIA agents—two Bolivians, Eduardo and Mario Gonzales, and a Cuban known as "Felix Ramos"—went out into the field trying to find people who would inform on the guerrillas.

"Ramos" was a Cuban exile, driven from his homeland by the Castro regime. Like many other Cubans in the CIA, he had been involved in the unsuccessful attempt to invade Cuba in 1961. Getting Guevara would be a small part of the revenge he and many other CIA men sought for their defeat at the Bay of Pigs.

There were small engagements. In July, Guevara's little band captured the village of Sumaipatra, took the uniforms from nine soldiers, and bought some medicine.

A few weeks later, the CIA agents were in Santa Cruz and a $4,600 reward was being offered for information leading to Guevara's capture. On Thursday, September 28, the guerrilla band was ambushed at La Higuera and three men were killed, reducing its number to eighteen.

Then, on Sunday, October 8, Che Guevara was captured at the Quebrada del Churo.

Guevara and his companion, Willi, were taken to La Higuera under guard and put in separate rooms in a schoolhouse.

The next day, Monday, the wound in Guevara's leg, which was not serious, was treated by a doctor. Several officers tried to interrogate Guevara, including one of the Cuban CIA agents. He would answer no questions about his companions or contacts in the world of rebels.

Later, Guevara asked to see the schoolmistress of the school where he was being kept.

"Ah!" Guevara greeted Señorita Cortez, "you are the *maestra*. You know that in Cuba there are no schools like this

one. We would call this a prison. How can the children of
the *campesinos* study here? It's antipedagogical."

"We live in a poor country."

"But the government officials and the generals have
Mercedes cars and plenty of other things. . . . That's what
we are fighting against."

"You come a long way to fight in Bolivia."

The *maestra* soon left, finding the interview difficult.

Later that morning, Guevara was visited by several
Bolivian generals, a colonel, an admiral, and a Cuban CIA
man.

According to former CIA official Victor Marchetti, the
Cuban CIA agent was impressed with Guevara. He had found,
he reported to CIA headquarters, that Guevara did not believe he was going to be killed. When "he finally realized that
he was about to die, his pipe fell from his mouth." He
quickly pulled himself together, however, and asked for some
tobacco. The CIA agent "clearly felt admiration for the
revolutionary and compassion for the man he had helped to
capture."

Guevara's death was probably not desired by the CIA.
The agency was smart enough to foresee his martyrdom but
could not halt the forces it had set in motion. Once Che was
captured, the government of President René Barrientos was
too fearful of his popularity among the students in La Paz to
keep him alive.

A few minutes after the Cuban CIA agent left the room,
at about one in the afternoon, a young officer, Lieutenant
Mario Teran, came in. He carried a carbine, a small rifle.
"Sit down," he said.

"Why bother? You are going to kill me."

"No—sit down."

He shot Guevara. Then another officer entered and shot
him in the neck with a pistol.

Then more officers came in and shot him.

At five in the afternoon, Che's body arrived in the town

of Vallegrande strapped to the runner of a helicopter. It was shown to newspaper reporters. The CIA agents had the body loaded into the back of a Chevrolet panel truck. One of them took the dead man's fingerprints, to double check his identification. For further proof, the head and hands were shipped to La Paz. The body was burned. No trace of it remains.

Here is what happened afterward. Che's diary, which had been found in a saddlebag two days after his death and had been kept in the hands of the CIA, suddenly appeared in Havana in July 1968. Then Antonio Arguedas, the Bolivian minister of the interior, who was secretly in the pay of the CIA and who was in charge of the Bolivian Intelligence Service, disappeared.

Minister Arguedas appeared in Chile to ask for political asylum. Instead he was handed over to the local CIA station. His case officer (Arguedas's contact with CIA headquarters) flew down from Washington to keep him quiet. Arguedas insisted on speaking out against the CIA and its activities in Bolivia. He denounced his government as a tool of American imperialism, said that other officials also worked for the CIA, and disappeared again.

Over the next several months, Arguedas appeared in London, New York, and Peru. He said that he had been the one who had released Che's diary. He had done this, he said, because he agreed with Guevara's aims. He also told how the CIA had recruited him in 1965. The agency had done this, he said, by threatening to reveal his radical student past. They had told him they would ruin his political career if he did not work for them.

Somehow, the CIA was able to talk Arguedas into returning to Bolivia to stand trial. But he told a *New York Times* reporter that if anything happened to him, Lieutenant Mario Teran, the executioner of Che, would release a tape recording with more details of his charges against the CIA and the Bolivian government.

Bolivian President Barrientos died in an accident the following summer. Shortly thereafter, Arguedas was gunned down while walking on a street in La Paz. He recovered and is now living in Cuba.

No tape was ever released, and all these events are suspicious. It is difficult to know the truth about anything involving the CIA.

Of the sixteen other men with Guevara on that fatal Sunday, October 8, ten got away. Five of them were later rounded up. Three of the Cubans escaped to Chile. Inti Peredo, the Bolivian leader of the other rebel band that Guevara thought was lost, was still fighting in Bolivia a year later.

Ernesto "Che" Guevara was a rebel, an insurgent, the most notorious insurgent in the world, brought to heel by counterinsurgents. His fall was a victory for the counterinsurgency program of the United States.

Che Guevara boasted he would start more Vietnams to destroy the United States, and the country he regarded as his archenemy destroyed him with Green Berets from Vietnam and CIA agents. The Green Berets trained the Bolivian rangers, and the CIA agents helped track Guevara down.

And yet, somehow, it was not really a victory. For now, as one travels in Latin America, from Mexico to the pampas or Argentina, Che's picture can be found everywhere among the poor. His well-known bearded face, beneath the beret of the guerrilla fighter, is seen on small wooden plaques hung by bus drivers over their heads. Photographs of his dead body are stuck on the walls of the *chozas* (huts) of *campesinos,* alongside pictures of saints of the church; and the words *¡Che vive!* (Che lives!) are scrawled on the sides of buildings.

Ernesto "Che" Guevara died on October 9, 1967; and yet he lives. He is the saint of many Latin Americans who see in revolution a cure for the condition of the oppressed.

If he was an enemy of such importance that the CIA

spent a lot of time and effort tracking him down, he was an enemy that the CIA, to a great extent, created.

He is an example of a strange phenomenon. That is, we create what we fear. The CIA, formed out of fear of communists and revolutionaries, made Che Guevara a communist and a revolutionary when it crushed the Arbenz government in Guatemala. We may be certain that there are others like him in many parts of the world. As the CIA raises up enemies where none existed, it, in effect, makes itself needed. The more communists and insurgents there are in the world, the more the CIA can claim to be needed to suppress them.

The final irony may be that in seeking to bring revolution to Bolivia from outside, Guevara was interfering with the politics of another country. He found himself no more trusted by Bolivia's Indians than any agent of U.S. "imperialism" and met a fate no different from what he would have wished on any CIA agent who set foot in Cuba.

Whenever there is an interest and power to do wrong, wrong will generally be done. —JAMES MADISON to Thomas Jefferson, October 17, 1788

The Unwitting Patsies

BACKGROUND

At the time the CIA was formed, Congress had gone to great lengths to make sure that the agency would not operate within the United States. To make certain that all it would do inside the country would be "collation of information gathered by other government agencies," Representative Clarence J. Brown and other critics insisted that the 1947 National Security Act prohibit the CIA from having "police, subpoena, law-enforcement powers, or internal security functions."

Despite this, incidents kept cropping up of CIA activities on the home front. In 1966, it raided the Georgetown residence of its employee, Hans Tofte, to recover secret documents that he was working on at home.

This break-in and others like it were against the law. In the first place, the agency is forbidden to exercise any police function within the United States. In the second place, no one, including government agents, can burglarize the home of any American for any reason. The matter could have been handled legally by referring it to the FBI, which does have domestic police powers. And the premises could have been entered with a search warrant obtained in accordance with the Fourth Amendment.

In 1975, the agency admitted to two more break-ins, also in connection with checking security infractions of its employees.

The reports of additional break-ins by the CIA were part of a whole list of illegal acts confessed to by DCI (Director of Central Intelligence) William Colby in January 1975, after the New York Times *had accused the agency of keeping files on 10,000 American citizens and of other violations of its charter. These included following American citizens inside the United States, wiretapping their telephones, surreptitiously opening mail and "inserting . . . individuals into American dissident circles."*

The Rockefeller Commission, appointed by President Ford to investigate these charges, substantiated them in a report issued in June. It found nine more break-ins, thirty-two wiretaps, and thirty-two buggings, confirmed the illegal opening of mail and added that the agency had also eavesdropped on overseas telephone calls. CIA employees were protected from prosecution for these and other crimes by a secret agreement with the Justice Department that permitted the agency to withhold criminal information in the interest of keeping its secrets.

The commission reported that the CIA's surveillance of American dissidents—antiwar activists and black power groups—had started at the request of President Lyndon Johnson and had flourished under President Nixon. When it began, its stated purpose had been to uncover links between American activists and foreign governments. When no such links were found, it crossed over the line to become an investigation of what was purely domestic political activity. At its height, Operations Chaos, secretly functioning out of the basement of

★ **137**

the agency's Langley, Virginia, headquarters, employed eighty-two people, thirty of them agents, three of whom infiltrated domestic groups. During its seven years of existence, Operation Chaos accumulated files on 7,200 American citizens and 6,000 others; and on about 1,000 organizations. It had indexed the names of 300,000 Americans.

A former CIA man told the New York Times *that more than twenty-five agents were assigned to New York City in the late 1960s to spy on antiwar activities at Columbia University and elsewhere. His work, he said, involved wiretaps, break-ins, and keeping files on student activists. "We'd go out and take some photographs, and follow them," the former agent said. "We had different I.D.s . . . flash a badge and say we were a reporter for a magazine . . . we'd usually use* Newsday. Atlantic Monthly *was another good cover—no one ever heard of it."*

Their excuse for watching the antiwar activists was that they were suspected of receiving money from the KGB, the Soviet secret police. Even if that were so, the CIA had no right to watch them. It was the duty of the CIA to report such suspicions to the FBI, which is authorized to perform counterespionage within the United States. By performing domestic counterespionage on its own, the CIA was violating the law.

The first indications most Americans had of the extent of CIA involvement within the United States came in 1964 with the publication of David Wise and Thomas Ross's book, The Invisible Government.

Then, three years later, it was revealed that what the CIA would find to do inside the United States would be limited only by its imagination. The story that follows describes a CIA caper that did not violate the charter directly, since it did not come under the heading of "police, subpoena, law-enforcement powers, or internal security functions." On the other hand, it very much surprised a number of congressmen who

★ **138**

had been told twenty years before that all the agency would be doing on the domestic front was putting together information, most of it from other government agencies.

In communist countries, everything is controlled by the government. Student groups, like all others, are linked to the government and must follow its policies. Students from communist countries, representing their student unions at international conferences, are not free to speak their own views.

In 1948, for example, the International Union of Students (IUS) refused to condemn the way students were treated when the communists seized power in Czechoslovakia. The IUS could not speak out because its members from communist countries were really government agents. Even some members from noncommunist countries followed the Communist party line because the Soviet government secretly supported their student unions.

When the IUS refused to denounce the Czechoslovakian communists, the National Student Association (NSA), representing American students, resigned in disgust. As representatives of a free, open, and democratic nation, the NSA would have no part in an organization that was not what it pretended to be. It wanted to be with other genuine student representatives, free to speak their minds, not with communist agents who were mere spokesmen for their governments.

Eighteen years passed. In 1966 the United States was in ferment. The civil rights movement was winning important victories and the war in Vietnam was violently opposed by students, who also objected to the military draft. In 1948, a large part of the world was appalled by the brutal way in which the Soviets destroyed the democratic government of Czechoslovakia. In 1966, a large part of the world was appalled at the brutal way in which the United States was terrorizing Vietnamese peasants.

The National Student Association, as the representative

of American college students, opposed the draft and the war in Vietnam and took part in the civil rights movement, which included condemning racism and colonialism in Africa.

The NSA sent representatives to an international student conference. Many of the members from other nations offered resolutions condemning the U.S. role in Vietnam and protesting racism in South Africa. At the conference, the NSA fought these resolutions, and as the most powerful member of the organization, did everything it could to prevent their passage.

The NSA representatives' stand at the international conference was the opposite of what its student members stood for. At the international conference, the NSA echoed the official policies of the United States government.

In 1948, the NSA condemned the IUS as a front organization masking the international communist conspiracy. Its members, said the NSA, were disguised KGB agents or their puppets and stooges.

In 1966, the Soviet student organization condemned the ISC, the International Student Council, attended by the NSA, as a front for American imperialism. Its members, said the Soviet Student Union, were American agents or their puppets and stooges.

The ISC was formed in 1949, the year after the NSA withdrew from the IUS. Originally consisting of NSA and student representatives from eighteen other countries, the new group grew quickly. Six years later, it had representatives from fifty-five countries, mostly from the new nations of Africa and from Latin America and East Asia.

By 1960, the NSA represented more than four hundred American colleges and universities. It was the most powerful group within the ISC and kept trying to get the members from underdeveloped countries to cool their demands that the ISC protest racism and colonialism.

In the fall of 1965, the NSA moved into comfortable headquarters in a four-story colonial house in Washington.

When a Washington *Post* reporter asked NSA President Philip Sherburne where the organization got enough money to pay the rent and staff of such a big building, Sherburne refused to give him any information.

The NSA was also paying the expenses of delegations sent to international conferences and providing hundreds of scholarships and considerable technical aid to student unions in poor countries. All this took quite a bit of money, more than the NSA could possibly have received as dues from members. This extra money came from foundations.

The members were never asked to choose those who would represent them at ISC meetings or at other foreign conferences. There always seemed to be students, or recent college graduates, in charge of the NSA who knew how to handle those things. Their decisions were rarely questioned.

The Foundation for Youth and Student Affairs (FYSA) in New York City gave about $300,000 a year to the NSA. Part of this went to pay the rent of the new headquarters and the salaries of its staff. The rest was used to subsidize the NSA magazine, the *American Student;* to help foreign students attend NSA conferences; to pay for some NSA technical-aid projects to poor countries; and to pay the NSA's dues to the ISC.

FYSA also provided funds for national student unions in other countries, as recommended by the NSA. One reason for the NSA's influence in the ISC was that it was actually supporting some delegations from other countries.

Other foundations that supported ISC programs were the San Jacinto Foundation, the J. Frederick Brown Foundation, and the Independence Foundation.

Early in 1966, Michael Wood, the NSA's director of development, whose job it was to raise funds for the organization, became worried. Wood had been on the NSA staff for a year. He had left Pomona College in his senior year to run a civil rights program in the Watts ghetto area of Los Angeles.

An NSA officer, impressed with what he was doing, had asked him to join the organization. As Wood started making efforts to raise the rather large sums of money that the NSA would need to run its programs for the coming year, he found the other officers very lackadaisical.

Wood thought that foundations being asked to supply hundreds of thousands of dollars would expect to receive carefully prepared proposals telling a great deal about how the money was to be spent. Instead, the other NSA officers handed in brief and vague notes concerning their needs. Wood was also annoyed because he had learned that Phil Sherburne, the president of the NSA, was negotiating with some foundations on his own. Wood didn't see how he could do a good job under those conditions. He finally told Sherburne that if he wasn't given complete charge of fund raising and the right to demand properly prepared proposals, he would have to resign.

Sherburne didn't want Wood to resign. He took him out to lunch and explained that the NSA didn't really have to worry about money because it worked with the CIA. Normally, Sherburne said, Wood would have been told about this when he became director of development, but the other NSA staff members and their CIA contacts didn't think he could be trusted with the secret.

Almost all the foundations that supported the NSA and the ISC, Sherburne explained, were just passing along CIA money. The Independence Foundation, the San Jacinto Foundation, the FYSA, the J. Frederick Brown Foundation, and the Sidney and Esther Rabb Charitable Foundation, Sherburne said, were all CIA fronts. The NSA had also received money from the Rockefeller Foundation and the Ford Foundation, but as far as Sherburne knew, this money did not come from the CIA.

NSA officers who were in on the secret used a special code language when talking of their CIA connections in front of others. They called the CIA the "firm," and those who worked for it, either as agents or as members of the NSA staff in the know, were called "witty." Those directly in the employ of the CIA, from Covert Action Division number five of the CIA's Plans Division, were called "fellas" or "boys."

The CIA "case officers" in the Plans Division were all former "witty" NSA officers. Other former "witty" NSA officers worked for the fake foundations. Harry Lunn, the executive secretary of the FYSA, was a former NSA president.

All the "witty" NSA officers had to take a national security oath which purported to make it a federal crime for them to reveal the secret relationship with the CIA. Sherburne was breaking this oath in telling Wood. The NSA officers received $3,000 "scholarships" to pay for their travel in foreign countries, even if they did no actual studying, and were also given draft deferments. When they returned from ISC meetings, or after visits to foreign countries, they gave the CIA reports on the student leaders they met so that the agency would know the thinking of those who were likely to become leaders of their countries in future years. These reports helped the CIA to recruit some of these leaders as American spies.

One reason that Sherburne was breaking his oath was that he was unhappy about the secret relationship with the CIA. As a matter of fact, it was his fault that Michael Wood was worried about funds. Normally, the CIA kept them well supplied; the fake foundations kept up a steady flow of checks. The flow had slowed lately because the CIA was trying to punish Sherburne. Sherburne had tried, unsuccessfully, to break away from CIA control by getting money from other sources.

The picture that Sherburne drew of the NSA was far different from the way Wood, and thousands of NSA members, supposed their association to be. They had thought it an independent group of students free to express their own ideas and act on them. Instead, it was run by a small inside group

Michael Wood, the National Student Association officer who revealed the CIA's connection with his organization. (*United Press International*)

pledged to secrecy by the CIA, taking orders from them in the field of foreign affairs, and getting in return money and such favors as draft deferments.

NSA's headquarters and staff, its monthly magazine, and the elaborate conferences it held for foreign students were all paid for by the secret spy organization. People posing as American student leaders were really operatives getting information on foreign student leaders and following the government line at international conferences. In a word, the NSA in important respects was little different from the student unions of the communist countries that it had long despised.

When Sherburne and the other officers of NSA found that Wood was giving the story to *Ramparts* magazine, they tried to get him to retract it. Wood's reply was that they

★ 144

should tell NSA members the truth. They refused to follow his advice, and so the first the world knew of the CIA's relationship with the organization was when *Ramparts'* February 1967 issue appeared.

Americans in general, including most members of Congress, were astonished at the amount of CIA activity that was taking place inside the United States. Not only was the CIA supporting a student organization with headquarters in Washington that operated on campuses all over the country, but *Ramparts'* story also mentioned a whole group of foundations with offices in the United States.

Up to then, Americans had always thought of foundations as private affairs, set up by wealthy individuals, or groups of individuals, to supply money for worthy purposes while providing the givers with certain tax advantages. But here were the Borden Trust in Philadelphia, the Price Fund in New York, the Kentfield Foundation in Dallas, the Edsel Foundation in San Francisco, the San Jacinto Foundation in Houston, the Beacon, Independence, the J. Frederick Brown and Sidney and Esther Rabb Charitable Foundations in Boston, and the Foundation for Youth and Student Affairs in New York City all serving as disguised pipelines for CIA funds.

With the information from Wood as a starter, *Ramparts'* reporters investigated these foundations to learn what other organizations they gave money to. It was found that dozens of other American organizations were supported by the CIA. These included the African American Institute, the American Federation of State, County and Municipal Employees, American Friends of the Middle East, the American Newspaper Guild, the Asia Foundation, the National Council of Churches, the National Education Association, Praeger Publishing Company, Radio Free Europe, certain labor-union activities, and a service that had sent hundreds of Americans to attend youth festivals in Helsinki and Vienna.

The CIA, through these foundations, was also supporting magazines and journals in many countries and the Congress for Cultural Freedom in Paris. The Congress, in turn, supported a number of respected journals. The editor of one of these, *Encounter,* was a CIA agent.

There was widespread criticism of this involvement of the CIA in so many organizations based in the United States and of its backing of what had up to then appeared to be independent organizations and magazines. This criticism was embarrassing to CIA Director Richard Helms who, just a short while before, had told the Senate Foreign Relations Committee that the CIA did not operate in the United States and did not use the American student-exchange program as a cover for spying.

Under attack for having so many CIA operations inside the United States, Director Helms asked a member of his staff to prepare a report on the agency's connections with American universities.

It took the executive director of the Agency months to compile the report which, eventually, was several inches thick. The CIA was paying many professors to do historical and political research, most of which would be kept from publication. In some places, entire departments and research institutes were at work on special research and development projects, designing new kinds of eavesdropping equipment, invisible inks, new lenses and photographic methods, and the like.

The Center for International Studies at the Massachusetts Institute of Technology was entirely supported by the CIA. A new building on the Michigan State University campus in East Lansing was built with funds from a project in Vietnam, part of which was a cover for five CIA counterintelligence experts.

Many professors also worked for the CIA as recruiters of foreign agents from among their foreign students.

The agency also supported seemingly independent research organizations like the Institute for Defense Analysis in Washington, to which Richard Bissell was sent when he was fired from the CIA for his part in planning the Bay of Pigs invasion.

At the time of the initial shock over the CIA's involvement on American campuses and its operations through foundation fronts, President Johnson appointed a three-man committee to look into the matter. The committee, one of whose members was CIA Director Helms, reported back that on the whole the CIA was doing a good job. All that happened was that the ways of supplying CIA money to the various groups was changed to make it harder to trace. The CIA claimed to be ending its ties with the NSA and some of the other groups, but how could one ever be sure, when those who honor the ties are sworn to secrecy?

Those NSA officers who "wittingly" worked for the CIA did so for a number of reasons. The CIA appealed to their ideals because many of the projects they supported in other countries were in themselves worthwhile. The CIA men told the NSA officers that they were helping causes they believed in, such as organizing progressive student unions in Africa, by accepting CIA money. The African countries, they explained, would not accept the money if they knew it was coming from the U.S. government.

NSA officers thought they were deceiving others in a good cause. There were material benefits, too: travel, money, access to jobs in the government—CIA jobs—and draft deferments. But is being deceitful in a good cause better than being deceitful in a bad cause? As Michael Wood noted in *Ramparts,* all of the "witty" NSA officers had to practice "everyday dishonesty, the need to clam up when in the presence of the 'non-witty' staff members, to fudge, to make excuses and deflect embarrassing questions. Perhaps a professional intelligence operative, who sincerely believes in anti-Communism at any price, can learn to suppress with not too much damage that most basic instinct of youth—to be open, frank, questioning of all things, in communion with his friends. But for the typical NSA staff member, part of a generation whose instinct is to mask hypocrisy, the compromise comes very hard indeed."

And what of all the other NSA members? As political scientist Marcus Raskin wrote, "The CIA made patsies out of thousands of young Americans who went abroad to conferences or who studied under NSA auspices, but who unknowingly were paid for, and were used by the CIA as contacts, covers and mail drops. Furthermore, how do we now face other nations who took us at our word that our students were 'free' and therefore different from the Communist-run youth groups? The CIA owes an apology to the innocent college students of this last generation."

Power always sincerely, conscientiously . . . believes itself Right. Power always thinks it has a great Soul, and vast Views, beyond the Comprehension of the Weak; and that it is doing God Service, when it is violating all his Laws.

—JOHN ADAMS to THOMAS JEFFERSON, February 2, 1816

The White House Burglary Gang

BACKGROUND

1761–1971: two centuries plus a decade. In 1761, the Boston merchants objected to the Writs of Assistance and John Adams listened to James Otis's arguments that Britons had rights that could not be disturbed by any British government. First came arguments heard by judges in robes of British scarlet; then, fourteen years later, arguments having proved futile, Massachusetts farmers were firing at coats of British scarlet.

Then came independence, the conquest of a continent, power reaching into every corner of the globe, and in 1971, the dreadful events described in this tale.

We had come full circle.

On Wednesday, August 25, 1971, two men checked into

a Los Angeles hotel. Ed Warren was a thin, sallow-faced man in his fifties with a thin, drooping mouth. George Leonard was younger and better built, with a military-looking black brush mustache.

That night they drove out to Beverly Hills, entered a building, and picked the lock of one of the doctor's offices. They were taking pictures when a Mexican cleaning lady entered. *"Yo soy un médico"* (I am a doctor), Ed Warren explained.

Ed and George were back in Los Angeles ten days later, with three other men. It was September 4, the Saturday of Labor Day weekend. Most offices would be closed for three days, until Tuesday, September 7.

Two of the new men put on delivery men's uniforms and carried a large green suitcase to the same doctor's office. The cleaning lady wouldn't let them in until they showed her Air Express invoices bearing the doctor's name. They left the suitcase in the office and punched a button in the door that would leave it unlocked.

Later that night, three of them returned. The three new men were skilled burglars. The door that had been left unlocked was locked. While one of them broke into the office, another listened to a small walkie-talkie radio. Outside, George Leonard was riding around in a car. If he saw police or anyone else coming, he would warn them by walkie-talkie. Ed Warren was several miles away watching the home of the doctor to make sure he didn't go over to his office and surprise the burglars.

Inside the office, the burglars opened the green suitcase and removed some special cameras. They were looking for papers. They picked the lock of the filing cabinet and looked through the records of the doctor's patients. It took longer than they expected. The papers they wanted weren't there. They took a few pictures of the open file drawer, packed the green suitcase, and left.

On Tuesday, September 7, 1971, Ed Warren and George

Leonard were back in the office from which they ran their burglary and other operations. Their office was in Washington, D.C., in the basement of the executive office building next to the White House. Ed Warren's real name was E. Howard Hunt. He had worked for the CIA for more than twenty years. George Leonard's real name was G. Gordon Liddy. He was a former FBI agent and an attorney.

The other three men who had joined Hunt and Liddy in Los Angeles were Bernard L. Barker, Eugenio Martinez, and Felipe De Diego. Barker was an American born in Cuba who had worked for the secret police of Cuban dictator Batista. After leaving Cuba when Castro took over, Barker had gone to work for the CIA. He had taken part in the Bay of Pigs operation and stayed in touch with the CIA while running a real estate business in Florida. Eugenio Martinez and Felipe De Diego were Cuban refugees who also had worked for the CIA; Martinez was still receiving a $100-a-month retainer.

The five men broke into the doctor's office under orders from John Ehrlichman, special assistant to President Nixon.

CIA agents study lock-picking and other ways of breaking into places as part of their training. According to former agents, FBI field agents also have committed burglaries in search of evidence in difficult cases.

Burglary was one of the things a CIA secret operator did as part of his work in other countries. The FBI, which only worked within the United States, was officially forbidden to practice burglary. Any agent performing a burglary, whether for the CIA or the FBI, would expect to be disowned if caught. According to former FBI Agent William Turner, FBI agents warned local police when they did a "bag job" so they would not be picked up.

The name of the doctor in Beverly Hills whose office was broken into was Lewis J. Fielding. Dr. Fielding was a psychiatrist. The White House was interested in one of the doctor's patients, Daniel Ellsberg.

Several weeks before the burglary, FBI agents had questioned Dr. Fielding about Ellsberg and he had refused to answer their questions. A doctor has a confidential relationship with his patients. A patient could never trust a doctor if there was a chance his secrets would be revealed to others. A psychiatrist—or any physician, for that matter—with a patient is like a priest hearing confession. To destroy trust would destroy the value of his work.

In the eyes of the White House, Daniel Ellsberg was a criminal who had stolen government papers and revealed secret information. Ellsberg had photocopied a secret Defense Department history of U.S. involvement in Vietnam and released a large part of it to the press, where it became known as the Pentagon Papers.

There were perfectly lawful ways of indicting him for these alleged crimes. And, in fact, Ellsberg was charged and tried for the crimes of stealing government papers and using them for his own purposes.

But in the view of President Nixon and his special assistant Henry Kissinger, Ellsberg wasn't just a thief, he was a threat to "national security."

Before Ellsberg left government service, he had worked for the National Security Council, where the most secret government policies are worked on. Dr. Ellsberg knew a lot about the nation's most closely held secret, the targets assigned to America's intercontinental ballistic missiles. He had helped prepare the list of rockets and their targets: the Soviet cities they were aimed at, and the sequence in which they were to be launched. Henry Kissinger knew what Ellsberg knew because he knew all the secrets. He was in charge of all U.S. secrets and secret operations.

There was no evidence that Ellsberg had given away any government secrets other than the Pentagon Papers, or that he planned to. Ellsberg claimed that he had given out the Pentagon Papers for patriotic reasons so that the American people could find out how they had been fooled by their secret government. Kissinger couldn't understand this. To him, patriotism meant keeping secrets, and the only reason someone would give them away was for money. He thought that Ellsberg had sold the Pentagon Papers to the *New York Times*. And if he had done that, Kissinger thought, Ellsberg would sell his country's most vital secrets to the Russians.

Besides this, in the minds of Mr. Nixon and Mr. Kissinger, the disclosure of the Pentagon Papers by themselves was a threat to national security. As they saw it, the disclosure of anything the government did not want known was a threat.

"Leaking" information, passing it on to others without proper authorization, is an old Washington practice. A government official will often tell a reporter about something on that reporter's promise he will not reveal his source. The official can often stop something he is against from happening, by alerting others in time for them to take action.

During that summer of 1971, someone leaked to columnist Jack Anderson news of how the administration was planning to help Pakistan in the war with India, while pretending to act neutral. Whoever leaked this information obviously disagreed with this policy and wanted to make it hard for the government to carry it out. There were also a number of other leaks that upset Dr. Kissinger.

All these leaks, the President and his assistants believed, threatened national security. There were laws to protect national security—laws against spying and against stealing government secrets or violating oaths of secrecy.

But the President believed that, beyond the laws, he had the right to say what threatened national security and what did not. "National security," in his view, embraced not just relations with other countries, but the concealment of the government's secrets from the American people. There was nothing in the Constitution that said the President could decide what national security was, nor did any law give him that authority.

Mr. Nixon and his assistants believed that when national security was involved, there was nothing the President could not do to protect the country. Mr. Ehrlichman, for example, did not rule out any crime as a means of protecting national security. "I do not know where the line is," he later told senators when asked if he could order people to be murdered.

When the plans to burglarize Dr. Fielding's office were being made, Liddy, a lawyer, told his secretary, Kathleen Ann Chenow, that the burglary would be unlawful if done by an individual citizen, but that "things of this nature" were not unusual for governments.

By seizing the authority to say what endangered national security, the President put himself into a position where he could do anything he wanted to any person he decided was a threat to national security. There is a word for such behavior by a ruler: despotism.

The President and his aides asked the CIA psychiatrists to give their opinion of Ellsberg's motives. The psychiatrists said he was patriotic. The FBI said that Ellsberg was not a spy. In spite of this, the White House insisted that Ellsberg was a security threat and put their own men, Hunt and Liddy, to work. They were nicknamed the "plumbers" because their job was to stop leaks.

Robert C. Mardian, Assistan Attorney General in charge of the Justice Department's Internal Security Division, gave the plumbers FBI reports based on the wiretapping of telephones of people who knew Dr. Ellsberg. Then they decided to break into Dr. Fielding's office.

The White House burglary team grew out of two trends. One was the growing power of Presidents to say what was good for the country and to act on their words. The other was the growing use of secrecy in government, and of secret operations. What was happening in the White House in 1970 and 1971 was that the men who ran secret operations for the United States against other countries started running secret operations inside the United States.

Men used to acting outside the law abroad no longer saw any reason to obey laws at home. The secret operator, Victor Marchetti and John Marks wrote in their book on the CIA, believes "that human ethics and social laws have no bearing on covert operations . . . the intelligence profession is free from all moral restrictions."

Men like Howard Hunt, who had broken laws as CIA operatives, could easily be persuaded that breaking into a doctor's office in California was in the best interests of their country. As he told U.S. Attorney Earl Silbert in 1973, Hunt did not believe the burglary was illegal.

"In your terminology," Silbert asked him, "would the entry into Dr. Fielding's office have been clandestine, illegal, neither or both?"

"I would simply call it an entry operation," Hunt replied, "conducted under the auspices of competent authority."

The line between what the CIA could do and could not do inside the United States was passed over most often when former secret operators like Allen Dulles or Richard Helms were in charge of the agency. The line was so ragged by 1970 that Central Intelligence Director Helms was willing to help Nixon's plan of wiretapping and bugging Americans.

And in the summer of 1971, after Presidential Aide John Ehrlichman asked the CIA to help Howard Hunt, it lent him equipment to use in the Beverly Hills burglary. At a "safe house," a secret CIA hideaway in Washington, Hunt was given a wig, a miniature camera disguised as a tobacco pouch, film, a tape recorder, alias documents, and a gadget to disguise his voice, to use on his first trip west to "case" the doctor's office. Later, the CIA processed the film.

The burglars found nothing. The wheels of justice turned. Dr. Ellsberg went on trial for illegal possession of the Pentagon Papers and the unauthorized conversion of them to his own use. The case against him was dismissed when the judge, Matthew Byrne, learned about the break-in of Dr.

Fielding's office and that Ellsberg had been overheard on a wiretapped telephone. Judge Byrne said that the government could not use illegal methods to gain a conviction.

Later, Presidential Aides John Ehrlichman and Charles Colson, plus Liddy, Bernard Barker, and Eugenio Martinez, were put on trial for the burglary. (Hunt and Presidential Aide Egil Krogh had already admitted their guilt.) They tried to evade the trial on the grounds that the burglary had been performed to protect the security of the nation. It was unfair to charge them with burglary, they said, unless it was first decided that national security was not involved.

Federal Judge Gerhard A. Gesell told them that national security could not be used as an excuse. "In approaching these issues," Judge Gesell explained, "it is well to recall the origins of the Fourth Amendment and the crucial role that it has played in the development of our constitutional democracy. That amendment provides:

" *'The right of the people to be secure in their persons, houses, papers, and effects, against unreasonable searches and seizures, shall not be violated, and no warrants shall issue, but upon probable cause, supported by oath or affirmation, and particularly describing the place to be searched, and the persons or things to be seized.'* [italics added]

"The Fourth Amendment protects the privacy of citizens against unreasonable and unrestrained intrusion by government officials and their agents. It is not theoretical. It lies at the heart of our free society. . . . No right is held more sacred.

"Indeed, the American Revolution was sparked in part by the complaints of the colonists against the issuance of writs of assistance, pursuant to which the King's revenue officers conducted unrestrained, indiscriminate searches of persons and homes to uncover contraband." Judge Gesell told how Massachusetts patriot James Otis's challenge of these unlawful searches by the king's officers "as a monster of oppression and a remnant of Star Chamber tyranny, sowed one of the seeds of the coming rebellion. The Fourth Amendment was framed against this background. . . .

"Thus the security of one's privacy against arbitrary intrusion by governmental authorities has proven essential to our concept of ordered liberty. When officials have attempted to justify law enforcement methods that ignore the strictures of this amendment on ground of necessity, such excuses have proven fruitless, for the Constitution brands such conduct as lawless, irrespective of the end to be served."

Judge Gesell went on to show that Ehrlichman, Colson, and Liddy had made no effort to obtain a search warrant that would have permitted them to enter the doctor's office legally. The defendants, the judge continued, had argued that the President's special responsibilities over foreign relations and national defense gave him the right to ignore the Fourth Amendment.

The judge denied that this was so, explaining that many of the important Fourth Amendment cases of the past had "concerned citizens accused of disloyal or treasonous conduct, for history teaches that such suspicions foster attitudes with a government that [cause it to violate] individual rights."

"National security" was no excuse for breaking into the homes or offices of private citizens. John Ehrlichman and the other defendants were convicted and sentenced to jail.

The most alarming aspect of the break-in of Dr. Fielding's office was that it only became public by accident. We would not know of it today, if the plumbers had not been caught pulling another job in the Watergate office building in Washington. They were caught red-handed, nine months after the Beverly Hills break-in, inside the office of the Democratic party's national chairman. Hunt and Liddy, and Barker and three fellow Cubans, were put in jail, and their connection with the White House was kept concealed for nine months until one of the burglars, a former CIA man named James McCord, revealed the group's links with Attorney General Mitchell.

The burglars, as secret operators, were pledged to silence, and the White House had such powers that it almost succeeded in hiding its role in the crime. The Fielding job in California only came out because the Watergate break-in was being investigated by the Senate and the President's powers of concealment were weakened.

Had the plumbers not blundered at the Watergate, their crimes would never have been discovered. Did they commit other crimes? Are other plumbers even now violating the constitutional rights of Americans?

We may never know and, indeed, may lose all our freedoms, unless we cease to allow our government to use "national security" as an excuse to cover up its crimes.

To suppose that any form of government will secure liberty or happiness without any virtue in the people, is a chimerical idea.
— JAMES MADISON in the Virginia Convention, June 20, 1788

Can Our System of Government Survive?

The direction in which this misuse of presidential power was heading was revealed in the Senate and House investigations that led to President Nixon's resignation in the summer of 1974.

The President used both the CIA and the FBI in attempts to conceal the link between the burglary gang and the White House.

The link between the burglars and the President was the cash they were paid, which was traced by the FBI to a bank in Mexico. The White House tried to keep it from being traced all the way back to the President by telling the FBI that investigating the Mexican bank funds would expose CIA operations, thus threatening national security.

This shows one of the dangers of government secrecy. It can be abused by an unscrupulous President to hide crimes. The secrecy cloak, added to the President's other powers, make it almost impossible to bring him to justice. For the President also controls the Justice Department, which investigates federal crimes, and the FBI.

Thus, while an assistant U.S. attorney in the Justice Department investigated the burglary, his superior, an Assistant Attorney General, told the White House what the U.S. attorney was finding out. And the acting director of the FBI was sending the White House its reports on the investigation. Those in charge of the burglary were also in charge of those investigating it, and steered the Assistant Attorney General away from the White House connection. The weak link in the plan was the burglars, some of whom knew enough to implicate the White House. If they all had remained silent, the President's guilt would never have come to light.

As instruments, the FBI and the CIA furthered the President's schemes in a number of ways. The acting director of the FBI destroyed files that might have revealed more illegal activities of the burglars. The CIA equipped the burglars and refused to pass on to investigators important information sent to it by James McCord, a former CIA man who had taken part in the Watergate break-in.

Had the President continued to use such powers unchecked by Congress or the courts, and had the FBI and the CIA continued to serve him, the American people would have lost their liberties as surely as if they had been conquered by a foreign enemy. They would have found themselves dominated by a White House that elected chosen successors by crippling the opposition and that levied tribute by fear. No man's home or possessions would have been secure and a twentieth-century James Otis who dared to speak out would have found himself discredited by the spread of fake information, if not jailed on some charge arranged by government spies.

If the two agencies are instruments of the President, then, clearly, we cannot hold them responsible for breaking laws without implicating the President who uses them. We see them then, as accessible tools of Presidents whose powers have passed constitutional bounds. (Other Presidents, including at least Franklin Roosevelt, John F. Kennedy, and Lyndon Johnson, had improperly directed the bureau to investigate congressmen and others critical of White House policies and to collect "intelligence for possible use against political opponents.")

But saying that the agencies are tools does not relieve them of all responsibility. Each agency, like any bureaucracy, has sought to grow and increase its power. As large permanent organizations full of career officers who devote lifetimes to their service, they have certain advantages over Presidents, cabinet members, and advisers who come and go every four or eight years. They have, to some extent, been able to free themselves from control by the President.

In 1908, Attorney General Bonaparte promised Congress that he would always know what every FBI agent was doing. A dozen years later, when the bureau had four hundred agents, Attorney General Palmer had to admit that he didn't know what the agents who rounded up the "reds" had been up to. He claimed that "the supervisory officers in the Department of Justice cannot know all that is being done by their agents." Even with his tight administrative methods, it is doubtful that Director Hoover, with more than eight thousand agents, knew what they all were doing. And the bureau, as we shall see, has found other ways of making itself independent.

The CIA, contrary to the intent of President Truman and Congress in 1947, has been making policy (as in Vietnam) and running large military operations involving thousands of men. It has achieved this by evading the restraints placed over it in the law. The act of 1947 that created the agency placed it under the control of the National Security Council (NSC). The exact wording of the law was that it operate "under the direction of the" NSC. This put the NSC, on which sat the secretaries of state and defense and other powerful government figures, between the CIA and the President.

To increase its power, the agency kept seeking to gain the ear of the President directly and to free itself from NSC control. It did succeed in gaining the President's ear in the early 1950s when it began submitting daily estimates of the world situation. With this briefing power, and a brother who was secretary of state, DCI Allen Dulles was able to have the NSC set up a small, friendly special group that cooperated with the agency rather than directed it.

By the time Kennedy became President, the agency had become so successful in evading the direction of the NSC that the Defense Department had no control at all over the attempt to invade Cuba at the Bay of Pigs in 1961. This, as CIA Executive Director Lyman Kirkpatrick later acknowledged, was the main cause of the Bay of Pigs fiasco. Had the Defense Department been in on the planning, it would have insisted that, if any invasion was mounted, it be accompanied by the air and naval support that would have ensured its success. It would not have agreed to the kind of half-baked plans used by the CIA.

What little public knowledge there was of the agency and its functions diminished as it assumed new tasks under secret NSC directives and presidential Executive orders. For example, one of these, National Security Council Intelligence Directive (NSCID) number seven, gave the CIA the power inside the United States to question Americans about foreign travels, and to pay universities to do research for them. (In some cases this would lead to universities acting as "covers" for CIA operations.) Many such directives and orders, we may assume, have been inspired by the CIA, which was able to get them implemented with the help of operatives it had placed in influential positions. By 1975, in the words of DCI William Colby, control of the NSC over the agency had been

The man with John F. Kennedy is Allen W. Dulles. It is November 20, 1960, a few weeks after Election Day. Dulles, then head of the CIA, has spent a whole day briefing the President-Elect on CIA secrets. By gaining direct access to Presidents, Allen Dulles greatly increased the CIA's ability to expand covert operations.   (*United Press International*)

reduced to "general guidance . . . through the Assistant to the President in National Security Affairs [Henry Kissinger]."

As they have become more powerful and self-directed, the agencies have achieved a frightening ability to stage-manage events. This gives them a capability of manipulating public opinion, which, in turn, can be used to increase their power.

Security agencies always try to dramatize the threats they are fighting in order to gain support. In 1914, when its main job was simply enforcing a law against carrying women across state lines for immoral purposes, the FBI tried to scare the nation into believing that the white-slave traffic was growing by leaps and bounds.

When it was given new powers against kidnappers in 1933, the FBI made it seem that the nation was overrun by kidnappers. Bank robbers and gangsters became a plague when the FBI was sent after them in 1934. By 1936, Director Hoover was warning the nation against the "armed forces of crime which number more than three million." Such warnings brought it increased appropriations from Congress, larger staffs, more buildings and equipment, and better pay. The FBI warned us against fascists in the 1930s, against communists in the late 1940s and 1950s, and against black power groups and Weathermen in the 1960s, growing bigger and more powerful year by year.

With *agents provocateurs* in its employ, an agency like the FBI can help make the trouble it is warning us against. If it can secretly stir up trouble by night, and quiet it by day, it has a formula for perpetual success. It will grow bigger and bigger until there is an FBI man on every block.

The CIA can similarly use *covert operations* to create an impression of trouble, and the need for *more* CIA operations, in any part of the world.

So we have agencies that have increased their power, that are far less under control than Congress planned, aiding and abetting superpowerful Presidents. When Presidents and their agencies exceed their just powers, is the fault theirs alone?

If so, we must conclude that the Constitution does not work. For it was designed to be a self-adjusting machine that would keep itself in balance. An Executive that exceeded the constitutional limits, it was thought, would be restrained by Congress and the courts.

Of course, the President was finally restrained by those other two branches. It was the threat of impeachment by the Congress and the courts' refusal to permit the President to withhold evidence that drove him from office. But they went into action when it was almost too late.

What would have happened to us had the burglars not been caught in the Watergate building? Has the system failed? Can our Constitution no longer safeguard our liberty?

To answer these questions, we must first look more closely at what is wrong. Is the President too strong, or is the Congress too weak? Are we to blame Presidents for expanding their powers, or the Congress and the courts for allowing them to?

If we follow the teachings of the founding fathers, we would place the blame more on the Congress than on the Executive. For the Executive was just doing what he was expected to do. Every power, the founding fathers knew, seeks to enlarge itself. There have been eras in the past when Congress has sought to run over the Executive, only to be checked at last by strong Presidents backed by Supreme Courts recharged by new appointments.

We have been living through an era, beginning at the turn of the century, when increases in presidential power have been generally welcomed by the American people. Strong Presidents such as the two Roosevelts (Theodore and Franklin), Wilson, and Truman were able to present every addition to their powers as weapons to be used against selfish special-interest groups while Congress remained too lazy or corrupt to defend the people.

A few members of Congress warned of the danger to the Constitution, while the great majority, following the passions of the moment, went along with the White House.

The growth in presidential power has come not in spite of Congress, but with its agreement, or at least its acquiescence. If presidential power is to be curbed, it can be done only by Congress.

The problem of the FBI and the CIA cannot be separated from this problem of presidential versus congressional power. Indeed, the excessive degree to which Congress has permitted the President to escape its supervision can be seen in the manner in which it has permitted the President's instruments, the FBI and the CIA, to escape its supervision.

Over the years, Congress has voluntarily relinquished its control over the FBI and the CIA. The budgets of neither agency are reviewed, contrary to Article I, Section 9 of the Constitution. Nor is there any control at all over their personnel, organization, or functions, as there is over every other agency in the government.

In the case of the FBI, the more than $300 million annual budget is approved as one lump sum, with the exception of four line-by-line items that amount to less than one-tenth of one percent of the total. The remaining 99.9 percent can be spent by the bureau as it wishes. The director makes an annual statement to the House Appropriations Committee in which he mentions accomplishments and projects plans, but there is no requirement that the bureau use the money in accordance with whatever plans are mentioned.

There are several reasons why the FBI is treated so carelessly. One is that it has a special status with the House committee that is supposed to examine its budget. The Appropriations Committee employs FBI agents as investigators for all its work. This puts the bureau in the unique position of working for two different branches of the government—the legislative as well as the executive. Another reason is that special files it has kept can be used to threaten congressmen with exposure of discreditable information or help them against political opponents.

Former Representative John J. Rooney of New York, when chairman of the Appropriations Subcommittee that handles the FBI budget, was always fulsome in his praise of the bureau. "There have been very few other agencies in government that have been so efficiently run and with such results to the taxpayers' benefit as the Federal Bureau of Investigation," he told a television interviewer in 1971. "Without a doubt Mr. Hoover is the greatest administrator we have . . . in any part of the government."

A report in the *New York Times* of February 25, 1974, indicated that the FBI had investigated those who opposed Mr. Rooney in primary elections in 1970 and 1972 and illegally passed along information for the congressman's use. The bureau had, apparently, been able to find nothing derogatory about Mr. Rooney's 1972 opponent, Allard K. Lowenstein, but it did find two small tidbits that Mr. Rooney mentioned in the course of his 1970 campaign against Peter Eikenberry.

In the case of the CIA, the situation is even worse. No part of the CIA's budget, which is more than twice as large as that of the FBI, is published. Congress permits the agency to conceal its budget in the budgets of other agencies; and Congress passed a law in 1949 exempting the agency from all laws regulating spending and allowing the DCI to spend money without even having to tell anyone else what it was for. Worse, it allowed the agency to decide what Congress should know about it. Having given away so much power, Congress has a hard time finding out much about the CIA.

In November 1971, during a debate, Senator Alan Cranston of California asked Senator Allen J. Ellender of Louisiana if he knew what the CIA was spending money on in Laos. Senator Ellender, who was the chairman of one of the two subcommittees that were supposed to check on the agency, said that he did not know.

"As you are one of the five men privy to [CIA] information, in fact . . . the number one man," Senator Cranston said, ". . . then who would know what happened to this money? The fact is, not even the five men [of the subcommittee] know the facts in the situation."

Despite Senator Ellender's admission that this was so, the Senate refused to limit the amount the government spends on intelligence operations.

Senator Robert A. Taft of Ohio saw clearly where this was leading in 1951, when he told the Senate, "The result of a general practice of secrecy . . . has been to deprive the Senate and Congress of the substance of the powers conferred on them by the Constitution." And four years later, a commission appointed by Congress to investigate the Executive branch warned that in giving up its right to review the "costs, organization, personnel and functions" of an agency, Congress was leaving the door open to "abuses of power."

To redress the balance, Congress is going to have to make some hard choices, and it is going to have to take a lot more responsibility. If it looks at everything the agencies do— as it is supposed to—then it will have to share the blame when things go wrong. We would expect, however, that a lot less would go wrong if Congress were doing its job. That is precisely the way our system is supposed to work.

We would expect that Congress would simply not permit the agencies to do things that violate fundamental principles. That's where the hard choices come in. Congress will have to point out to the FBI and the CIA that national security means, above all else, preservation of our Constitution.

FBI Director Clarence M. Kelley, for example, may stress the need to investigate "radical domestic groups," as he has in the past, because "to ignore the extremists' threats would be to gamble recklessly with the lives and freedoms of the citizens we serve." In support of this position, he may cite statistics, explaining, for example, that in 1974, there were 2,041 actual and attempted bombings in which 24 people were killed and 206 injured. In his view, such statistics demonstrate that extremists are a serious problem.

It is terrible that anyone is killed or maimed by a bomb, and such statistics are persuasive. But Congress would have to weigh the damage done by the FBI in trying to prevent such bombings against the damage done by the bombs.

For instance, in the name of not gambling "recklessly

with the lives and freedoms of the citizens we serve," the FBI harassed many people who had never made or planned to make a bomb. Many of these were the sort of fearless, free-thinking people who founded this nation.

Is the work of more than two thousand FBI agents and thousands more informers, infiltrating hundreds of organizations and watching tens of thousands of Americans, harming our constitutional rights to free speech and assembly more than our society is harmed by 24 bomb deaths and 206 injuries?

It is not easy to weigh damage to life and limb against damage to our constitutional rights; but we, and Congress, do so all the time. For example, in the year that those twenty-four people were killed by terrorist bombs, at least a hundred times as many were killed in muggings. If the FBI can justify spying on Americans for the purpose of keeping a few of us from being blown up by bombs, could not our local police justify all sorts of drastic measures to prevent muggings and other violent street crimes? They could, for example, keep streets and buildings under twenty-four-hour television surveillance or send out plainclothes decoys to beat up assailants.

We do not allow such measures to be taken because the benefit, safe streets, is considered not worth the cost, limitation of freedom. The fact is, freedom is always a gamble. The streets of Moscow are safer than those of New York. We could go even further than the Soviets, and prevent almost all crime, by installing a "Big Brother" system that would watch everyone.

It is up to Congress (and the people it represents) to measure the costs of FBI programs, in terms of freedom, against the benefits, in terms of security.

Congress will also have to apply similar tests to everything the CIA does.

One of the primary duties of the agency is trying to gauge threats to our security by collecting information about other countries so that we can judge their intentions and capabilities. The collection of information, whether by radio, reading, from spies, or from satellites orbiting the earth, hardly conflicts with the Constitution. The cost is in dollars rather than ideals, and the task for Congress would be the simple one of seeing that we get our money's worth.

But what about covert operations? These are justified by the CIA and the national security establishment on the grounds that, since they are practiced by our adversary, the USSR, we must do them too. The argument runs like this:

(1) The USSR tries to undermine other governments so that they will come under their influence. (2) If another government comes under the influence of the USSR, it will do things that hurt the United States. (3) When this other government hurts the United States, we will have to send in a military force: marines or paratroops, to protect our interests. (4) Clandestine operations can prevent steps 2 and 3. They are justified because it is better to struggle for influence secretly than to have to send in the marines.

Agents of the KGB, the principal Soviet intelligence group, are active in every country in the world. Their aim may be anything from stirring up a demonstration against American policies to arming guerrilla fighters or financing a coup against a country's rulers. KGB agents, often posing as Soviet diplomats, carry cash into countries to support their Communist parties. They have smuggled arms to the terrorist wing of the Irish Republican Army. In recent years, the KGB has organized plots against the governments of Egypt, the Sudan, Tunisia, Yugoslavia, and even Communist Poland and Cuba; it has been caught training guerrillas in Mexico and bringing money to Colombian rebels. In 1971, Great Britain expelled 105 members of the staff of the Soviet embassy when it uncovered their plans to blow up military installations and poison the water supply. Without a doubt, the USSR does try to undermine and influence other governments. Proposition 1 of the argument is true. What about propositions 2, 3, and 4, as they are used to justify covert CIA operations?

That communist governments will always be hostile to the United States (proposition 2), is doubtful. A good example of another government coming under the influence of the Soviets, as we feared, was China. In recent years, Communist China and the Soviet Union have been enemies. We should have learned years before, when Communist Yugoslavia broke with Russia, that communism does not make two nations allies any more than capitalism does.

It is also doubtful that we will be forced to take military measures every time our interests suffer (proposition 3). The Arab states hurt America when they raised the price of oil in 1973. We did not send in the marines.

Clandestine operations, as in Iran and Guatemala, have prevented other governments from coming under Soviet influence (proposition 4). But against this benefit (dubious in such cases as China) we must weigh the cost of arousing the hatred of those in whose country we are meddling.

The other price of secret operations is that they violate the principle of accountability to the people. If the American revolutionists objected to "taxation without representation," what would they think of paying taxes to support wars started without their consent?

Interfering with other countries is also against our principles. We have long claimed to believe that all nations have the right to choose their own destiny, a principle enshrined in the United Nations Charter, which, as a treaty, has a weight equal to anything in the Constitution.

Ideals and constitutional principles are empty words if we do not follow them. If the CIA smuggles funds to political groups in other countries, trains and backs police and military forces, and organizes plots against governments in Syria, Ecuador, Zaire, and Greece, if it helps fight rebels in the Congo and Peru, trains torturers in Brazil, supplies funds to

THE **FBI** AND THE **CIA**

Chileans striking against the Allende government, and assassinates foreign leaders, how is it to be told from the KGB? How is the United States to be told from the USSR?

At the end of the first chapter of this book, we asked if American democracy could tolerate the FBI and the CIA.

Recent experience has demonstrated that it cannot tolerate them in their present form, for they are not properly accountable to the Congress or the American people.

Can we tolerate them in any form? In other words, is it necessary to abolish them in order to preserve our Constitution?

The answer to this question is "No." Were they limited to the kinds of functions assigned to them by Congress, they would be safe enough. It is the activities and powers they have acquired through the years, often in secret and under questionable authority, that have made them the menace they are today.

But we should also ask ourselves why these two agencies have become so dangerous when other secret federal groups, like the Secret Service, have remained relatively harmless. The reason is that the FBI and the CIA function in the area of national security, an area that arouses strong emotions and is closely involved with politics and power.

We must recognize that national security agencies, because of the political penalties for being on the wrong side of a national security issue, always possess a potential for abuse. At the same time, we must recognize that we cannot do without them. For there are real threats to our security, and if we did abolish the two agencies, we should soon be devising others to take their place.

What Congress could do is to confine the FBI and the CIA to their lawful functions and divide them up into a number of smaller agencies. The FBI could be split into at least three separate agencies: one for keeping criminal records, another for catching interstate criminals, and a third for counterespionage. The CIA could be broken up into two agencies: one to gather information from all open sources, a second to engage in spying to get information abroad from secret sources.

Smaller agencies would be easier for Congress to control. But Congress would still have to exercise strict supervision to keep them within the confines of the law. The counterespionage mission of the FBI should be carefully defined, and the bureau should not be permitted to place any person or group under surveillance without the approval of some sort of civilian watchdog group and without a special court order.

In the case of the CIA, all covert operations should be abolished as contrary to what we stand for. Nor should the agency undertake any activities at all without the full knowledge and consent of at least two committees of each house of Congress and without the written authority of the President and his Secretary of State.

The Congress has already moved in this direction by requiring that all secret CIA operations be reported to the Senate beforehand, with proof that they have been approved by the President.

Legislation alone, however, will not end abuses. The law, as we have seen, did not prevent the CIA from acting as domestic police. There must be respect for the law. The CIA agent who had been spying on Columbia University students told a *New York Times* reporter that he "knew what the charter was." Like E. Howard Hunt, he was following orders from his superiors.

Obedience to superiors is necessary in all organizations; but no other mortal, or group of mortals, should always unquestioningly be obeyed. A person must have a higher authority in himself, higher than anyone he serves. A free person is responsible. He makes choices between right and wrong. Unless he does so, he becomes a slave to a system that, in the name of all sorts of virtues, will perform unspeakable evils.

This is what Madison meant when he said that the new government would not work without "virtue in the people."

Is there virtue, or are these the final days of a noble experiment in "government of the people, by the people and for the people"?

The outcome remains in doubt. It always will. Freedom, the right to personal belief, the maintenance of individual dignity against the power of governments, corporations, and other combinations of men, has never been safe.

Our destiny, finally, depends on each one of us. Unless we guard our heritage, we shall surely lose it. Said Sam Adams in 1776, "If ye love wealth better than liberty, the tranquillity of servitude better than the animating contest of freedom . . . crouch down and lick the hands which feed you. May your chains set lightly upon you, and may posterity forget ye were our countrymen."

Bibliography

Books about the FBI

The FBI Story by Don Whitehead, foreword by J. Edgar Hoover. New York: Random House, 1956.

    The "official history" of the FBI written with Director Hoover's cooperation. An interesting book with considerable inside information, particularly concerning the director's relationship with President Roosevelt at the time when political surveillance of Americans began anew under Hoover, after a lapse of a dozen years.

The FBI Nobody Knows by Fred J. Cook. London: Jonathan Cape, 1965.

    An anti-FBI book that balances Whitehead's account. Cook compares the bureau's image with its actual performance and finds Hoover personally responsible for FBI excesses, particularly red-hunting.

The FBI in Our Open Society by Harry and Bonaro Overstreet. New York: W. W. Norton, 1969.

    This purports to be a balanced account in which critics like Fred Cook are taken to task; however, it tends to ignore the real failings of the bureau.

Hoover's FBI by William W. Turner. New York: Dell, 1971.

    A former agent's view of the FBI as a bureaucracy dominated by the whims of Director Hoover. It has many insider anecdotes that give the flavor of what it was like to be a working special agent.

Investigating the FBI, edited by Pat Watters and Stephen Gillers. New York: Ballantine, 1973.

    This book is based on a conference held at Princeton University in October 1971, attended by attorneys, law-enforcement experts, writers, political scientists, former FBI agents, and Justice Department officials. Director Hoover refused an invitation to attend. The chapters, based on lectures and discussions at the conference, present the most complete, balanced appraisal of the bureau available.

The Federal Bureau of Investigation by Max Lowenthal. New York: William Sloane, 1950.

A one-sided anti-FBI book with, however, interesting documentation on the very early days of the bureau.

J. Edgar Hoover, The Man in His Time by Ralph de Toledano. New York: Arlington House, 1973.

A one-sided pro-FBI book with, however, interesting insights into Hoover's beliefs, based on the author's personal relationship with the former director.

Books about the CIA

The Invisible Government by David Wise and Thomas B. Ross. New York: Random House, 1964.

This book is a landmark, the first popular presentation of CIA operations and CIA influence on American foreign relations.

The Espionage Establishment by David Wise and Thomas B. Ross. New York: Random House, 1967.

Here is revealing information on the intelligence operations of several different countries.

The Pentagon Papers as Published in the New York Times. New York: Quadrangle Books, 1971.

The secret history of the Vietnam war that Daniel Ellsberg photocopied. It is a long book with many actual CIA and Defense Department cables and documents. The interpretive essays by *New York Times* staff members are excellent; with them the reader can make sense out of the "papers" themselves. This collection provides a unique view of the Secret Team at work. It should be mentioned, however, that Colonel Prouty, who was part of the team, says that the papers were selected with a view toward making the CIA look good at the expense of the Defense Department. Accurate intelligence *estimates* are accented, while the *secret operations* that contradicted the estimates are given little attention.

The Secret Team by L. Fletcher Prouty. Englewood Cliffs, N.J.: Prentice-Hall, 1973.

A book written hurriedly, in white heat, by a former air force colonel and Secret Team functionary who had come to feel that the CIA was a menace to the United States. One thing he is angry about is that the CIA, in defending itself against responsibility for the Vietnam debacle, is trying to pass the blame on to the armed services. The urgency of the book carries it along, despite some repetition, and it is full of insider details on how secret operators function at the higher levels.

Bibliography

The CIA and the Cult of Intelligence by Victor Marchetti and John D. Marks. New York: Knopf, 1974.

Marchetti spent fourteen years in the CIA, Marks worked in the State Department's Intelligence bureau. Marchetti and Marks know what they are talking about. Passages censored from the book by the CIA are left blank, adding to its fascination. Some of the information is new, and the picture they present is of an agency that, through secrecy, has gotten out of control and no longer functions according to the intentions of Congress in 1947.

Sources

Chapter 1. Drug raids, *New York Times,* April 3, 1974; February 6, 1974; March 6, 1974. Hoover profile, *New Yorker,* Jack Alexander, September 25, 1937; October 2, 1937; October 9, 1937. CIA, *New York Times,* October 23, 1974. Lori Paton, *New York Times,* January 28, 1974. William J. Sullivan, *New York Times,* December 1, 1974. CIA history, *New York Times,* December 26, 1974. "Army Bares Files on Spying in U.S.," *New York Times,* June 14, 1975.

Chapter 2. See books about the FBI listed earlier.

Chapter 3. Charges of Illegal Practices in the Department of Justice, Subcommittee of the Judiciary, U.S. Senate, Congressional Record, 1923, pp. 3005-25; Report of the Subcommittee, pp. 56-63. *Portraits and Portents* by A. G. Gardiner, New York, Harper, 1926.

Chapter 4. "The Days of Suspicion," D. Lang, *New Yorker,* May 21, 1949. *U.S.* v. *Remington,* 343 U.S. 907; 208 Fed. 2nd 567; brief by Joseph Rauh, R. Green, and D. Pollitt, U.S. Supreme Court October term, 1953, government rebuttal and reply brief. *The FBI Nobody Knows* by Fred J. Cook, chapter 10. *J. Edgar Hoover, The Man in His Time* by Ralph de Toledano.

Chapter 5. *New York Times,* March 29, 1975; February 10, 1968. *The Orangeburg Massacre* by Jack Nelson and Jack Bass, Cleveland, World, 1970. *Investigating the FBI,* edited by Pat Watters and Stephen Gillers, pp. 177-8.

Chapter 6. *Investigating the FBI,* chapter 9. *Menard* v. *Mitchell and J. E. Hoover,* 430 F 28, 328 F Supp 718. *New York Times,* October 21, 1971.

Chapter 7. *The FBI and the Berrigans* by Jack Nelson and Ronald J. Ostrow, New York, Coward, McCann & Geoghegan, 1972, pp. 234, 332.

Bibliography

New York Times, May 1, 1971; March 1, 1972. *New Yorker,* July 25, 1970. Trial of Vietnam Veterans Against the War, *New York Times,* August 1- September 1, 1973.

Chapter 8. See books about the CIA listed earlier.

Chapter 9. *The U-2 Affair* by David Wise and Thomas B. Ross, New York, Random House, 1962. *The CIA and the Cult of the Intelligence* by Victor Marchetti and John D. Marks. *The Secret Team* by L. Fletcher Prouty, pp. 197, 334, 355. *New York Times,* May 6, 1960; May 7, 1960; May 8, 1960.

Chapter 10. *The Secret Team. The Invisible Government* by David Wise and Thomas B. Ross, chapter 10. *The CIA and the Cult of Intelligence.* "I Quit," Sergeant Donald Duncan, reprinted in *Ramparts,* Vol. 7, No. 10, 1969. *Viet Cong: The Organization and Techniques of the National Liberation Front in South Vietnam* by Douglas Pike, Cambridge, Mass., M.I.T. Press, 1966. *New York Times,* May 7, 1970, et seq. *The Last Crusade: America in Vietnam* by Chester Cooper, New York, Dodd, Mead, 1970.

Chapter 11. "A Dire View of the United States from Abroad" by Arnold Toynbee, *New York Times,* May 10, 1970. *Che Guevara* by Andrew Sinclair, New York, Viking Press, 1970. "The Execution of Che by the CIA," Michèle Ray, *Ramparts,* March 1968. *The CIA and the Cult of Intelligence,* chapter 4. "Diary of Che Guevara," *Ramparts,* July 27, 1968.

Chapter 12. "A Short Account on International Student Politics and the Cold War, with Particular Reference to the NSA, CIA, etc.," by Sol Stern, Michael Wood, Marcus Raskin, *Ramparts,* March 1967. *The Espionage Establishment* by David Wise and Thomas B. Ross. *The CIA and the Cult of Intelligence. New York Times,* January 6, 1975. Rockefeller Commission report, *New York Times,* June 11, 1975.

Chapter 13. *New York Times,* January 17, 1974; May 22, 1974; May 25, 1974. Gesell decision, *New York Times,* May 25, 1974. Ehrlichman authority, CIA role, July 3, 1974. *Newsweek,* May 14, 1973. *Time,* May 14, 1973. Silbert, etc., *New York Times,* May 9, 1974. *The CIA and the Cult of Intelligence.*

Chapter 14. *Mexican Money—The Great Cover Up* by B. Sussman, New York, Thomas Y. Crowell, 1974. Cointelpro, *New York Times,* May 16, 1974; November 14, 1974; November 16, 1974. National security, *New York Times,* March 7, 1974. Policy of lying, *New York Times,* November 23, 1974. Army spying, *New York Times,* September 19, 1974; November 9, 1974. Chile, *New York Times,* September 17, 1974; October 17, 1974; October 21, 1974. Lies, Helms, *New York Times,* January 22, 1975; January 23, 1975. Senator Church, *New York Times,* September 12, 1974;

Bibliography

September 17, 1974. CIA domestic spying, *New York Times,* December 22, 1974 to January 20, 1975. IRS spying, *New York Times,* December 8, 1974; November 18, 1974. Senator Sparkman limits CIA, *New York Times,* January 7, 1975. Secret budget, *New York Times,* December 12, 1974; January 13, 1975. CIA inquiry, *New York Times,* December 10, 1974; January 9, 1975. FBI inquiry, *New York Times,* January 21, 1975. Colby statement, *New York Times,* January 15, 1975. "The KGB Plays Dirty Tricks, Too," R. Conquest, *New York Times,* September 22, 1974. KGB, *New York Times,* February 20, 1974; January 19, 1975. "CIA Is Reported to Have Helped in Trujillo Death," *New York Times,* June 13, 1975. *The Imperial Presidency* by A. M. Schlesinger, Jr., Boston, Houghton Mifflin, 1973.

Index

Index

Index

Index

353.007
MUN   **Munves, James**

                The FBI and the
                CIA

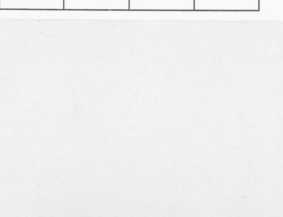
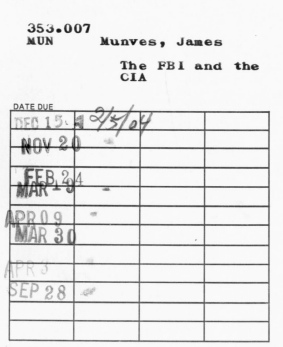